A Word of Welcome

Welcome to PARABLES OF JESUS, a study of nine of Jesus' stories of faith to the people of faith.

The parable is perhaps one of the most popular and easily accessible learning tools. Jesus told stories frequently. They seemed simple enough on the surface, but a careful hearing revealed deep truth and convicting challenges for those who took the story seriously.

We invite you to invest yourself in a study of these ancient and timeless parables. Who among us is not concerned about love and forgiveness as well as welcome and responsibility in our chosen or given family? Cast a glance at the parable of the father and his two sons. How many of us are attentive to the need for growth in a purpose that has meaning and effectiveness? See the parable about the mustard seed.

In each of the parables you will find an explanation of the story and of the context in which it was told. Insightful commentary provides some direction on what the story might mean for you today. Learners will also be encouraged in each session, if it seems appropriate, to make or reaffirm a commitment to Jesus Christ.

PARABLES OF JESUS is a self-contained study with all the teaching/learning suggestions conveniently located on or near the main text to which they refer. In addition to your Bible, all you need to have a successful group or individual study session is provided for you in this book. If you wish to dig deeper, there are some instances in which you will be invited to look up Scriptures, words, or concepts in a Bible commentary or dictionary.

Most of the discussion and reflection questions are addressed to "you," since learners and leaders will have the same book, which can be used in a group setting or for personal study. Some of those questions invite the group members to discover what the Bible or the session text says and means. Others ask for some analysis or imaginative thinking. Some ask for learners to tap their own experience, to think about what it meant and how it felt to them, and what the results were. The parables consider what happens to the "good guys" and to the "bad guys," and some of the reflection questions will push you to think about how you might relate to both.

We invite you to delve deeply into this ancient font of Jesus' teachings and to open yourself to their transformational power.

PARABLES OF JESUS

by J. Ellsworth Kalas

ISBN 0-687-05621-7

This book is printed on acid-free paper.

01 02 03 04 05 06—10 9 8 7 6

MANUFACTURED IN THE UNITED STATES OF AMERICA

ABINGDON PRESS

Contents

Meet the Writer

A native of Sioux City, Iowa, J. Ellsworth Kalas received his bachelor's degree from the University of Wisconsin (1951) with a variety of honors and his Master of Divinity degree from Garrett-Evangelical Theological Seminary (1954) with distinction. He has received honorary doctorates from Lawrence University (1965) and Asbury Theological Seminary (1986).

Dr. Kalas served thirty-eight years as a parish pastor. The first twenty-two years were in Wisconsin, the next sixteen years at the Church of the Saviour (United Methodist) in Cleveland, Ohio.

In July, 1988, Dr. Kalas became the associate in evangelism with the World Methodist Council, with an emphasis on spiritual renewal in local congregations and special programs for clergy.

On July 1, 1993, Dr. Kalas became the first Beeson Senior Pastor in Residence at the new Beeson School of Preaching at Asbury Theological Seminary, Wilmore, Kentucky. In this role he serves as teacher and mentor to the Beeson Scholars and as adjunct professor in the D.Min. program.

Dr. Kalas is a frequent contributor to religious publications. He serves as a video lecturer for Disciple Bible study and assists in training leaders for the Disciple program. Dr. Kalas is also the author of numerous books published by Abingdon Press.

The Story of Two Foundations
Matthew 7:24-27

Session Focus ■

Everybody agrees that our culture is too often superficial and prone to shortcuts. Give attention to translating easy acquiescence and woeful head-shaking into substantial commitments. Emphasize the very practical aspects of building on the rock, and especially to celebrate the reality and the challenge of dedicated following of Jesus Christ.

Session Objective ■

This session should help us to see the difference between "wise" and "foolish" living and to recognize the unique power of Jesus as Savior and as Teacher in leading us into truly "wise" living.

Session Preparation ■

Tap into the convictions that group members already espouse. They won't need, in many instances, to be convinced about building their lives on rock. But they will need to find the spiritual energy to go from comfortable agreement to effective living. Take time for reflec-

All Jesus' parables are drawn from the common experiences of life. He delivered the very mysteries of eternity in the guileless garb of shepherds and tradespeople, homemakers and farmers.

But never more so than in the parable that is now before us. Not only was Jesus drawing his story from a common experience of village life, he was taking it from the world he knew best. Jesus had grown up in the home of a builder. We generally speak of Joseph as a carpenter; but in that world a carpenter was also likely to be a stonemason and a bricklayer—that is, an all around builder.

The same thing is often true in a small town or rural community in our day. A man with a knack for building may, with his helpers, pour the concrete, build the house, put in the plumbing and electricity, and decorate the finished product. It was even easier in Jesus' day when there were no building codes to be met—none, that is, except the judgment of the customer.

tion and introspection on your own commitments. In the course of this week, watch for examples of the two kinds of living: building on sand and building on rock. Watch news stories and commercials on television, read the newspaper, and listen to casual conversations. Such contemporary, down-to-earth examples will make this lesson more powerful.

Session Outline ■

Choose from among these activities and discussion starters:

Ancient Homebuilding ■

Review how homes were built and furnished. If you have access to pictures in a Bible dictionary or other resource, use them as a visual reference.

Ancient Home Building

Palestinian homes were generally simple, although the wealthier residents might have two floors and build on higher ground overlooking their neighbors. Single-room homes provided housing for the entire family as well as for their animals, although a four-room style was often typical. The largest room extended the length of the entire house giving access to three smaller rooms. Often the living quarters for the family were in a raised terrace where they cooked and slept. Animals were kept in a section below the terrace that provided some shelter for them at night. They were fed from mangers, which could be dug out of the terrace floor or made from clay or stone and placed in the below-terrace level.

These simpler homes were constructed of mud bricks held together with a kind of plaster. Floors were usually packed earth, perhaps mixed with ash, with waterproof lime plaster to seal out moisture. Some would have straw or leather mats for area coverings.

Roofs generally were constructed of poles cut and laid across the walls about one yard apart. The openings were covered with branches or with a hardened mixture of clay, straw, and lime. After a rain, the roof had to be rolled with a stone cylinder to repack the surface and keep it from leaking. Other roofs were made of clay or tile. The roof area was sturdy enough to entertain guests or to be used for an extra sleeping area. In the hottest time of the year, the roof might serve as both living room and bedroom.

More ornate homes might be constructed around a central courtyard and have either one or two floors. Among the wealthiest and grandest homes in Palestine, some covered over 2000 square feet. The courtyard could be enclosed fully or partially, but it might also be open to the sky. In some, the roof was supported by columns. Homes for the well-to-do could be made from cut or field stones or fired bricks. Occasionally these homes would have wood paneling, although wood was too scarce to be used extensively.

Cisterns were carved from the bedrock of the grandest homes, a convenience unavailable to the ordinary citizen. Sunken ovens were another amenity of the wealthy. Most homes used a cylindrical clay mound less than three feet in diameter, open at the top and scraped out in the middle.

Some homes had raised ledges for sleeping or sitting. Individual beds or chairs were rare for most, but houses often had chests and closets constructed of wood and used for storage. Families also had wooden ladders to ascend to the roof if there were no steps, a table, and a few stools.

A Secure House

A Secure House

Read Matthew 7:24-27. Have on hand a Bible commentary on Matthew for extra information.

How well do you think one of these ancient homes would have stood up to a heavy rain? (Remember that in very dry areas, rain tends more to run off than to soak in.)

Discuss both the literal and figurative dangers of when "the rain fell, and the floods came, and the winds blew" (7:25). What are some of the inevitable "floods" of your life? When have you been tempted "to build on sand"?

Jesus knew what he was talking about when he referred to "a wise man who built his house on rock" (Matthew 7:24). One imagines listeners nodding knowingly to one another, recalling that they have seen this teacher build or have heard of his doing so. He has good credentials for talking about building.

Most of the people listening to Jesus had at one time or another seen this scenario unfold in their area. They had watched someone pick a nice piece of land during the dry days of summer, the best time for building. The most attractive sites were often in sandy hollows. In the long, dry season, such an area looked ideal. But when the rains came, the sandy hollow could within hours become a torrent of water. Areas nearest the coast received the most rain, desert areas the least. The western hills of Galilee averaged about thirty-five to forty inches of rain per year (similar to New York), while the Jordan Valley or Sinai might have eight inches or less (similar to Arizona).

I understand this better, now that I live in Kentucky. As a midwesterner, I thought people were just being quaint when they said, "I'll see you tomorrow, the Lord willin' and if the creek don't rise." Then I found out about creeks. We bought a home with a creek running through the back yard—a lazy stream, two feet wide and six inches deep, that hardly showed a current. But one weekend a series of heavy rains changed our creek into a small, roaring river that overflowed until it surrounded our home on three sides.

That is the kind of scene Jesus describes, and everyone in the crowd recognizes it. They have seen these flash floods that can turn a pleasant home site, often made mainly from earth, into a muddy disaster area. Not only have they seen it, many of them have lived through it. It was simply part of the hazard of living. Nowadays such hazards are greatly reduced by flood control programs and sophisticated engineering, although even today floods can confound our best efforts. But in Jesus' time such flash floods were commonplace, unavoidable, and to be taken for granted.

So the secret was not only to build in a safe place—there were not enough of them. The secret was to build well enough that if such a disaster came, a person's house would survive.

And that is the issue of Jesus' story. A wise man, he said, builds his house on rock. Only a "foolish man" would build his house on sand.

Jesus' story takes for granted that floods will come. I do not want to build a philosophical system on an incidental part of the story, but our human experience proves that the point is a significant one. It is possible in

Talk about the strengths of life that are found in personal Christian faith. When have you been able to build and live on rock?

our day, in most areas, to build a house that is safe from flood waters. But it is not possible now, nor has it ever been, to build a life that will escape all storms. The floods *will come*. Their form may be financial or psychological; they may come in a doctor's report or in a lawyer's brief; or they may interrupt us in a shrieking of brakes and twisting of steel on a busy highway. But nobody gets through life without some storms. The issue, therefore, is to build well. The floods will come at some time or other, in one form or another, so be ready.

A Common Sense Story

Compare and contrast the two builders and the choices they made. What part do you think indifference or inattention plays in making choices about what is built and how?

A Common Sense Story

So this is a common sense story. It is not an eerie journey into arcane wisdom but something so down to earth that it ought to seem unnecessary. Yet millions of destroyed lives and tens of millions of destructive experiences indicate that we have not grasped common sense. So we have to be reminded again, and in a very direct, graphic way.

The story is indeed graphic. We watch two men building their houses. One carefully selects a foundation of rock; the other quite thoughtlessly builds on sand. I think that it is not that he chooses to build on sand; it is only that he is inattentive or indifferent. No one would choose to build on a poor foundation—especially in a land like Palestine, where rock is everywhere.

And so it is, of course, with our lives. No one chooses to be an alcoholic or a failure (however we define that term) or an obnoxious person. We get there by little steps and by accumulated bad choices. And usually those choices are made without serious thought of consequences. The person who built on sand was probably distracted from even a superficial soil analysis by other fac-

What do you think about the way we get to unwanted or dangerous consequences? What "little steps and bad choices" have you accumulated? In retrospect, what other choices could or might you have made to build a better foundation and achieve a better result?

What part, do you think, does hurry play in our decisions? What part does distraction play?

tors—nearness to the market, perhaps, or the view of a mountain or the presence of some trees. Our bad choices—the choices that harm or even destroy us—are often made when we are distracted by secondary matters. Effective living demands concentration.

I wonder, too, how big a part *hurry* played in the foolish builder's error. Is it possible that he saw the nature of the soil but chose to ignore the potential problems because he was in a hurry: He had to build now (or so he thought), and at the moment this was the only land available? I suggest this possibility not only because it could so easily have been the case but also because it points out one of the most troubling characteristics of our time. We are a quick-fix people. We want our solutions, our gratifications, our securities, in a hurry. And while some gratifications and some of life's easier solutions can be gotten quickly, true security is a long-term project. There are no short cuts to a really good life. Conversion itself may come in a moment, but Christian character has to be nurtured over the years.

I think I will also accuse that ancient foolish builder of being naive. Now in a sense, "naive" is only a rather specialized synonym for "foolish." The man in our story was naive about matters of building. He may well have been very knowledgeable in other matters; but when it came to choosing a site for his house, he was Mr. Innocent.

What is the place for innocence or naiveté in our faith? in our daily business routine? in our relationships? What potential consequences do we reap as a result of behaving or deciding naively or innocently?

Our contemporary culture often finds the truly good person to be rather amusing. If you are disturbed by profanity, by crude humor, or by shady business or political practices, someone will soon tell you how naive you are.

But no one is more naive than the person who thinks he or she can build life's house on the shoddy standards of compromised morality.

We can sometimes win a ball game by cheating, achieve some business success by bending the rules, or triumph in an election by lying about our opponent. But all these shady procedures are shifting sand. To build a life, we need rock.

Do not be intimidated by someone who calls goodness or a sensitive conscience "naive." The ultimate naivete is the assumption that we can build a substantial life out of shoddy material.

The Wise Way

What is suggested here as "the ultimate naivete"? How do you respond to that suggestion? Why?

The Wise Way ▪
Using the text and a Bible dictionary, define *wise* and *foolish* as those terms are understood in the Bible.

What is the wise person's secret? Well, we had better begin with a definition of the key word, *wise*. We face a difficult defining process under the best of circumstances because wisdom is such an intangible concept. Our definitions are likely to wander all over related areas such as education, knowledge, skill, and technique, to say nothing of contemporary concepts like "street smart."

But that is only the beginning of our problem. In order to do justice to this biblical term, we need to pursue a biblical understanding of the term. That is, we should not impose a late twentieth-century definition on this word. We had better find out how people used the word in Jesus' day and then apply that understanding to our own times. The basic principles are as good in one century as in another, but we need to know the meaning of the words we are using.

The Hebrews had tremendous regard for wisdom, but they saw it in very practical ways; it was never simply theoretical knowledge. When Bezalel and Oholiab (Exodus 31) were assigned to do art work in gold, silver, and wood for the Tabernacle, their talents would seem to us to be in the realm of craftsmanship; but the biblical writer describes them as having

What are some biblical examples of theoretical wisdom? of practical wisdom?
What are some contemporary examples?

wisdom or divine spirit. The writer of Proverbs describes four things on earth that are "small, yet they are exceedingly wise": ants, badgers, locusts, and lizards (Proverbs 30:24-28). The measure of wisdom, to put it simply, is the ability to do well with one's particular role in life. It is a very pragmatic outlook.

I expect that the biblical writers, if talking about family life, would hold up as their standard of wisdom, not a lecturer on child rearing, but a parent who had raised several children successfully. The measure of wisdom was in the doing, not in the philosophizing. So it is that the man who built a house that could withstand the storms is seen as a wise man.

Hearing and Acting ■

Look up the references to "hearing" (other than in Matthew 7). Note that "hearing" does not depend on our ears but on our comprehension.

In what ways does God communicate with us? In what ways do you recognize that God is communicating with you?

Hearing and Acting

The wise man in Jesus' parable is someone "who hears these words of mine and acts on them" (Matthew 7:24). Have you noticed how much the Bible makes of the act of hearing? So often the Hebrew prophets began their messages with the phrase, "Now hear the word of the Lord." When the prophet Ezekiel had the vision of his nation as a valley of dry bones, he was nevertheless told to "speak" to them. When Jesus explained his parable of the sower (Matthew 13:18-23), the constantly recurring word is "hear."

Perhaps this is the Bible's way of telling us that God is a communicating God. We humans are paid the high compliment of being perceived as creatures with whom God communicates in some language or fashion and that have the capacity to understand and to respond. God does not control us like puppets; we are spoken to because we are reasoning creatures.

But having received, the test is in whether we will act. A few days ago I said, in a public lecture, that I sometimes get frustrated by the passing of years because I see so many things in the Bible that I want to preach about, teach about, or write about. As I examined my soul a few hours later, I realized that I had missed the heart of the matter—and I had done so in a way that is all too easy for a teacher-preacher-writer. I might better be worrying that I will not have time in my life to act upon all that I learn from the Scriptures. For that is the issue of our knowledge of the purposes of God, that we shall act upon what we know.

In the course of my work I spend a fair number of nights in hotels. I am fascinated by the size of the training industry; I sometimes wonder how hotels would survive if it were not for the thousands of training programs that are held every year by every imaginable kind of business. We are constantly on the stretch to make better salespeople, managers, technicians—and yes, better Christians. The same phenomenon is evident in the publishing field; there is apparently no end of books on better parenting, on personality improvement, and on money management.

But in truth, most of us already know a great deal more than we put into practice. We go to conferences and read self-help books in the hope that we will come upon some brilliant new information that will do for us what has never been done before. Most of the time, however, we know enough to be and do much better than we are now doing. It is not more knowledge we need; what we need is more commitment. Blessed are those who hear the word and act upon what they have heard.

Building on the Foundation

On the other hand, I am impressed that it is so often those who know the most and who are doing the best who still seek to know more. Several years ago I was giving a series of

When have you discovered that you knew more than you thought you did about a matter of importance? How did that realization help you act on what you knew?

What barriers to faithful action do you face? What can you do about them? How do you mobilize help? How do you feel about relying on someone else? (Remember that Jesus' teachings affirm interdependence.)

Building on the Foundation ■

What are the ways the Bible encourages you to grow in faith? What motivates you to increase your biblical and faith foundations?

lessons on prayer for a church in Kentucky. Every day a retired minister, nearly ninety years old, found his way to the class. I was quite sure that he knew more than I did; but in his wonderful humility and hunger, he came to each class and listened with an intensity that brought forth my best efforts. He was eager to hear and to act. No wonder his life was built on rock!

What are some of the trappings that we use to deceive ourselves into thinking that we have a "strong house" that is really built on sand?

Because I love knowledge and because I think God meant for us humans to keep on growing, I can get enthusiastic about any effort at personal improvement. But I have my prejudice; I am prejudiced in favor of eternity. As much as I hope that people will improve their minds, develop their social skills, and pursue better health practices, all these fall into the shade compared with the issue of growth in Christ. I have no argument with insurance salespeople; some of my best friends are financial consultants. But I am troubled that so many people buy health, accident, life, auto, and disaster insurance but give hardly a thought to their souls. After all these transient matters are past, you and I will still be eternal souls, required to check out our accounts with heaven.

And that is the essence of this parable. It is altogether possible that the house the foolish man built was attractive and well-appointed by the standards of his day. All of that meant nothing when the rains came and the winds blew. All that mattered then was the foundation on which the house was built. How could a person be so shortsighted, so *foolish*, as to be excited about a building's architecture and adornments when it was built on sand? And how can we spend so much of our time and enthusiasm on things that pass away, while neglecting the one thing that matters?

Are there weightier matters that need your attention?

Jesus, Teacher and Savior ■

What does Jesus suggest in this parable is what matters the most?

Jesus, Teacher and Savior

But what is it that matters most? So many voices clamor for our attention, so many issues claim to be the bottom line, so many philosophies purport to be the way. In the midst of them all, one quiet but insistent Voice says, "Everyone then who hears *these words of mine*" [italics added] (Matthew 7:24).

I wonder how audacious that statement sounded when Jesus first spoke it. Here was a relatively unknown teacher from a backwater community who was daring to say that his words were a matter of life and death! As far as his immediate audience was concerned, he was only a few months removed from building and repairing houses in the village of Nazareth; and now he was saying that he was the authority on building the ultimate house of a human life.

How authoritative are Jesus and Jesus' words in building the "ultimate house" of your life?

Jesus' claims still have to be taken on faith today. But faith does not have to make quite as big a leap. For nearly two thousand years, people have been putting his teachings to the test; and the results are really quite awesome. Mind you, not all of us who call him Lord do him worthy credit. But those persons who take Jesus most seriously have produced lives that prove his words to be true. The honor roll of great believers whose names are known is legion, but the full list of wondrous believers is beyond counting. I have preached in hundreds of congregations in my lifetime, but I have never been in a church of any denomination for three days without finding someone (and usually several people) I felt should be added to the honor roll of great human beings—true saints, that is.

What is the main point Jesus is teaching in this parable? What does that mean to you?

This is because Jesus was not simply a purveyor of good advice. Advice is always cheap, and even good advice is not hard to come by. Jesus offered more. Those who came to know him recognized that he was

What, for you, is the difference between Jesus' good news and good advice?

the Savior as well as a teacher. Of good advice we had plenty; Jesus came to bring good news, the gospel.

I think it is interesting that this parable comes as the conclusion to the Sermon on the Mount. Whether the Sermon on the Mount was preached in the consecutive form in which we have it in Matthew 5–7 or whether the author of the Gospel brought together key pieces of Jesus' teaching in this one powerful collection, this parable becomes its climax. It is as if Jesus were saying, "After you've heard all my challenges—the Beatitudes, the statements on murder and adultery, the teaching on prayer, the warnings against worry, and the advice about the wide and the narrow gates—now, what are you going to do? Will you build your life on what I have said, or not?" It is really that simple—and that demanding, too.

Seen as a kind of conclusion to the Sermon on the Mount, what new interpretation or insight comes with this parable?

The Parable and Me

This parable is really a kind of evangelistic sermon. It is what the evangelist would term an altar call or what the liturgist might identify as the invitation to Holy Communion. It says, "You've heard the teaching? Now what are you going to do about it?" That is, we are right back to the key verbs of the parable: everyone who hears and acts or who *hears* and *does not act* (Matthew 7:24, 26).

This parable can be acted upon in two ways. The first is a climactic decision, where one chooses in a completely life-altering way to follow Jesus Christ. We think of this sort of decision more often with persons whose lives are dramatically out of control; those are the conversion stories that are most often told.

But persons who have grown up in the church can also experience conversion. Roman Catholic priests sometimes refer to the conver-

The Parable and Me ■

What are, or can be, the consequences of hearing and acting versus hearing and not acting?

Have you had what you would describe as a conversion experience? If so, what was it like? What has been the result?

sion of the baptized, that is, the conversion of those who have passed through the rites of the church but who truly accept Christ as Lord only after they become young people or adults.

Then there is the continuing conversion of the faithful. Those of us who gladly acknowledge that Jesus Christ is our Lord discover that we must often make choices that reinforce our initial decision. To put it in the language of our parable, we return to the rock for times of recommitment to that which matters most.

This lesson gives extraordinary opportunity to remind ourselves of the root issues of life. Our culture can so easily tend to the superficial, to the quick-fix, to the easy way out. This lesson reinforces values that last.

If you wish to affirm or reaffirm your personal decision to "build your house on rock," offer your prayer of commitment.

Close With Prayer ■

Receive prayer requests; and after praying for these special matters, join together in this prayer:

We gladly acknowledge you, O Lord, as the Rock of our salvation. We are grateful for strength in our times of weakness, for faith when we are inclined to be uncertain, for depth when it would be easy to be shallow. Grant that our faith may be so strengthened that we will provide strength for others so that, by your grace, we may bring rock into someone else's uneasy life. In Jesus' name we pray. Amen.

Session Two

The Sower
Mark 4:1-20

Session Focus ■

This lesson is aimed specifically at believers. Some parables are directed at people in general, and some to the scribes and Pharisees; but this parable is for disciples. Particularly, this parable is intended to help us in our calling to sow the seeds of faith in the field of the world.

Session Objective ■

The primary purpose of this study is to help us become more faithful and hopeful witnesses to our faith. This involves becoming convinced that we are meant to be sowers and getting a realistic expectation as to the problems we face.

Session Preparation ■

Before group members arrive for this session, put four headings on the chalkboard or poster paper for the different kinds of soil. During the discussion, encourage group members to describe these soil types by contemporary experiences or examples.

Most teachers want to work in settings that are considered conducive to learning. We want a comfortable, well-lighted, properly air-conditioned or heated room. Special visual aids should be available. Interruptions are kept at a minimum so nothing will intrude upon the relationship of teacher and student.

Jesus of Nazareth had no such advantages.

His classroom was a hillside or a seashore. His students paid no tuition—beyond the crucial matter of their time and attention. Jesus posed no registration or admission requirements. Any wandering man, woman, or child who was curious enough to pause and listen was thereby enrolled. How surprising that history's most important lessons were offered under such limited circumstances and that Jesus is described, even by the religiously indifferent, as the greatest teacher who ever lived!

How did Jesus do it? What was his method?

The big secret, of course, is an intangible one—the person of the Teacher himself and the anointing of God's Spirit that rested upon him. But the tangible factor of method is easier to identify. As the crowds gathered around him, the Gospel writers tell us, he "began to teach them in parables." Parables were one of Jesus' unique teaching tools.

Session Outline ■

Choose from among these activities and discussion starters.

What are Parables? ■

Define *parable* in a way that everyone will understand. See if anyone can suggest some present-day equivalents of the parables. Are some comic strips or editorial cartoons, for example, a variation on the parable form of communication?

Planting Seeds ■

Discuss briefly what you know about gardening, farming, planting, and harvesting. If you have had no personal experience, mention what information has come to you through other sources.

Review and compare the differences between ancient farming and today's farming (or gardening) practices. What are the difference? the similarities?

What Are Parables?

A parable is a story with a point. A parable is usually brief; some of Jesus' parables are hardly more than two sentences. A parable uses some commonplace object or incident to shed light on that which is utterly uncommon. A parable's aim is to make a bewildered person say, "Ah! Now I understand." An effective parable is as likely to get that response from an illiterate person as from a professional scholar. At its best, a parable gets past barriers of age, education, and culture. And because a parable is a story, it is quick to capture our attention.

Thus I see Jesus looking out one day on a somewhat skeptical crowd. He smiled for a moment, then said, "There was this farmer not far from here . . ." And quickly the people gave him their attention.

Planting Seeds

As this farmer (or sower) was sowing his seed, Jesus said, some seed fell along the path where the birds ate it. Some seed fell on rocky places where the soil was shallow; while this seed sprang up quickly, it died just as quickly once the sun grew hot. Other seed fell among thorns. But though the soil was good, the thorns gradually choked out the plants. But some seed fell on good ground where it produced crops at thirty, sixty, or a hundredfold.

This was a familiar scene to the people of Jesus' day, but some of the details are not so immediately clear to us. A first-century farmer planted his seed before plowing the ground, not after. Thus he sowed it broadcast, scattering the seed freely over all kinds of soil. Some farmers used a simple labor-saving device. They put a sack of seed on the back of a donkey and cut a hole in the corner of the sack so the seed would drain out as the

Read or summarize the parable about the sower. Where did he plant his seeds? What happened to their growth? (*Do not spend a lot of time with this now; it will be considered in different ways throughout the session.*)

How do you interpret Jesus' comment about the parables, that some may listen, but not understand? Explain why you agree or disagree with the text's suggestion about what Jesus meant salvation to be.

The Nonproductive Planting ■

Encourage free imagination about what constitutes hard soil, shallow soil, and thorny ground in our contemporary society. This will help to make the lesson come alive and become more practical.

donkey walked up and down the field. By either method, the seed was deposited in a rather haphazard fashion.

Though the setting for the story was clear enough to the disciples of Jesus, they had trouble with its meaning. When the crowds were gone, these disciples asked Jesus for an explanation. Jesus prefaced his interpretation with what seems to be a hard word. Quoting from the prophet Isaiah (6:9-10), Jesus said that he spoke in parables so that people

> may indeed look, but not perceive,
> and may indeed listen, but not understand;
> so that they may not turn again
> and be forgiven. (Mark 4:12)

On the surface, this sounds as if Jesus wanted his teachings to confuse people rather than to enlighten and save them. Obviously this is not the case, for such would be contrary to the whole mood of Jesus' life and to the very reason for his coming into the world.

Commentaries give a variety of explanations. The simplest and most likely explanation is found in the language and style of the Middle Eastern world, where points are often made by exaggeration and dramatic overstatement. To put it simply, I think Jesus is saying, "Salvation is a gift, but you will have to pay attention to receive it. If you do not care enough to listen and to apply yourself, you will miss the good gift of God, even though it is freely available." Then Jesus addressed the parable itself.

The Nonproductive Planting

The farmer is one who sows the word of God. Some people's lives are like paths where the seed cannot make even a temporary entrance. As soon as they hear the word, the adversary comes and takes it away.

All of us know people like that. Indeed, we may remember times when our own lives were in just such a state. We were so "trampled upon" by the commerce of life, by people and circumstances, amusement and career, or tragedies and economic worries that God did not receive even a thought.

As a pastor, I have often heard such a word from people in their early thirties who return to the church after being away since their mid-teens. They were "so busy" in college (fun, books, and dating) and then in establishing a career—perhaps with a good deal of moving about—that eternal matters never seemed to enter their minds. Whatever imitations of eternity fell upon their lives were picked up by the "birds of the air" before any impression was made.

On another point in the spectrum, some persons are so inundated with dilemmas of how to pay for the basic necessities of life, care for a parent or child who is desperately ill, or deal with life's dramatically unfair battles and losses that they have scant time to think about "discretionary" activities such as dressing up and going to church.

Yet others have been betrayed by the church and find that they cannot disassociate hearing the word of God from hearing what seems like hypocrisy or deceit within the institution. Before the Holy Spirit can plant a seed to root, the opportunity is lost.

The seed that falls on rocky places, Jesus said, describes those people who hear the word and receive it. But, "they have no root, and endure only for a while" (Mark 4:17).

Again, you and I have known such persons. They are people of quick enthusiasms and equally quick indifference. Some of them move like quicksilver through cults and spiritual fads, moving always with a flash of

What reasons or excuses have you heard that have kept persons from productive growth in their faith life? Which ones have you used or been tempted to use? What has been the effect?

How do you determine when pursuit of religious or spiritual matters is *not* discretionary, but necessary?

Reflect on how to "sow productive seed" for someone who has felt betrayed or been injured by the church. If this has happened to you, what was most helpful?

What are some current examples of shallow ground? quickly evaporating but exciting fads?

excitement. In some cases they show the same shallowness in other aspects of their lives, including career and friendships. They are the kind of people who say, with excitement, "Hey, I've just come upon the greatest book! It's changed my whole outlook on life." But if you ask them about that "greatest book" six months later, they may have a hard time recalling that they even read it. Or they may report that they have now found something even more wonderful.

Their ground is shallow. Because it is shallow, anything that comes their way springs up quickly. But also because their ground is shallow, new life can find no depth of sustenance. "When trouble or persecution arises...immediately they fall away" (Mark 4:17). New Christians, especially, may be vulnerable, not because they are shallow, but because their faith is not yet mature. Those "veterans" in the faith have a special responsibility to model, to mentor, and to encourage all other believers in the disciplines and practices that allow seeds of faith to grow, descend deep roots, and thrive.

The third setting for the seed seems particularly descriptive of our times. "And others are those sown among the thorns; these are the ones who hear the word, but the cares of the world, and the lure of wealth, and the desire for other things come in and choke the word, and it yields nothing" (Mark 4:18-19).

What are some current examples of thorny ground? If this soil can be productive, what can you do to pull out the thorns? If you have found yourself tenuously rooted in thorns, what helped you to a more spiritually productive place?

I am struck by the fact that this soil is probably as productive as any; that is why the thorns do so well there. It is the kind of soil one finds in many a modern, middle-class American. These are attractive, able people whose lives are full of activity. Further, the activities are likely to be generally worthwhile—perhaps a bit trivial at times, but not destructive. These people live well: nice home, relatively new car, a well-manicured yard, opportunities to travel, perhaps a club membership or a boat.

But Jesus described these things as "the cares of the world." And they surely are. The more we have, the more there is to worry about, the more to go wrong, the more to be insured against theft. If you and I were to take inventory of the time our minds are preoccupied with worry about the "things" in our lives, we would probably be startled by the results. We set out to accumulate possessions, and we find that the accumulation possesses us.

How would you describe your own "cares of the world" and "lures of wealth"? What place does preoccupation have in this description? What can we do when the cares are or seem to be beyond our control?

Jesus referred also to "the lure of wealth." Perhaps the most deceptive thing about wealth is that we expect it to give more satisfaction and security than it is equipped to provide. Someone said, "I've been rich and I've been poor; and I can tell you, I'd rather be rich." Most of us would agree. But most of us have also discovered that possessions do not bring much lasting satisfaction. You and I are made to relate to persons and to God, not to things. Things make good servants, but things make poor friends and worse masters. Yet things have the power of deception.

Perhaps nothing is more threatening to our spiritual growth than the danger that we will be preoccupied. We may not think of our automobiles, boats, artwork, sports, and community involvements as being "thorns." But if they become so dominant in our lives that they choke out our communion with God, they are thorns indeed. Possessions and activities need not be evil in themselves in order to fulfill an evil end. Even the most attractive and worthwhile thing becomes a thorn if it crowds out that which is primary, our relationship to God.

We live in a complex society in which our relationship to God and many of our values are challenged as never before. It seems we can take little for granted. The "cares of the world" and the "desire for other things" may also refer to the numerous legitimate claims on our time, relationships, and wallets. Our cares may be tied up in addictions, fractured relationships, broken dreams, troubled children, or a myriad other heartbreaks. When God seems strangely silent, though in saner times we acknowledge God's everpresence, the thorns of doubt and despair choke out our hope and reason.

The Plentiful ■ Harvest

Interpret the four kinds of soil in light of your own life experiences. Do you recall a period when your own life was hard or shallow? To what degree do you feel as if you are in a fruitful state at present?

The Plentiful Harvest

Jesus' parables almost always end on an upbeat, positive note. And so it is with this one. Some seed, he reports, falls on good soil. This represents those who "hear the word and accept it and bear fruit, thirty and sixty and a hundredfold" (Mark 4:20). The farmer whose labor seems to be wasted on so much of the soil gets his return at last. And what a return it is. The abundance seems to make up for all the seed that produced nothing at all.

Let us remember, though, how fragile life can be, even a faithful life. The farmer with an abundant yield has plowed, weeded, toiled, and tended. This is hard and dedicated work. He has also been blessed with rain and the proper tools for tilling, which we might today interpret as the support of family, friends, and sufficient education and opportunity. A good harvest never happens by accident.

What are the "proper tools for tilling" that yield a plentiful spiritual harvest?

Thinking About the Parable

In reading and discussing this parable, we tend to put most of our emphasis on the non-productive soil. Of course it can be argued that the parable itself gives three times as much attention to the seed that fails. In truth, we often seem inclined to analyze our defeats more carefully than our achievements.

Thinking About ■ the Parable

Seek practical ways in which we can become more effective in sowing the seed of faith. Nearly every Christian wishes she or he could encourage faith in others, but we don't always see our opportunities nor do we feel that we have the courage or wisdom to use the opportunities that come to us.

What does "hearing and accepting" mean to you? What do you think, did it mean to Jesus?

An unfortunate sign of our times is the willingness many of us show to discount our young people. We focus on young people who have gone wrong (or whose methods and approach to life are different from our own) while we do little to discover the secrets of those situations in which those same individuals are going right. In addition to the lessons we might learn ourselves, we will all also benefit from finding out why so many teenagers and young adults are turning out well and applying that knowledge to marginal and troubled youth.

So too with this parable. How did some of the seed prove to be so wonderfully productive? Or more specifically, what is the secret of the good soil?

Jesus gives only the least hint, but that hint is significant. The fruitful soil represents those who "hear the word" and "accept it." The phrase "hear the word" seems almost elementary, but it reaches to the heart of the matter. Paul tells us that "faith comes from what is heard" (Romans 10:17), that is, from what falls significantly on our minds. We often look look upon faith as a mysterious guest, but Paul doesn't seem to think of faith this way; we get faith from what captures our awareness, he says. If what we "hear" is the voice of riches and the cares of this world, as in the case of the seed sown among thorns, our faith will settle on those things. If our faith is to be in God and in God's word, we will have to listen to the word, even if our lives are heavy with burdens and distractions.

Listening to the word is not easily accomplished in our time. Perhaps it never was. But in truth, distractions are more insistent and more continuous today than they have been at many times in the past. If we are to

Pair up and list the typical distractions in a typical day that deflect you from thinking about, witnessing to, or cultivating your spiritual life. What do you want to do about those distractions? What can you do?

hear the word, we will have to push our way through the barriers and daily needs that press upon us from every side. Hearing the voice of eternity amid the demanding clamor of the present is difficult.

Having heard, we must also *accept*. Much of our faith problem may come from not hearing the word clearly enough to make an informed decision. But sometimes after we have heard, we resist. Our lives are as hard as a trodden path or shallow from living superficially or badly encumbered with the cares and worries of this world to the point where we simply will not accept the gracious offer of God.

But when people hear and accept the word, the harvest is astonishing. And the glory of the harvest often has little to do with the apparent quality of the soil. I think of the magnificent beginnings of the Protestant movement in Europe. Among them were Calvin, Luther, and later the Wesleys. They did not plant their seed in the most attractive territory of those days. To the contrary, they often worked with the downtrodden masses whose lives were bordered on one side by poverty and grinding labor and on the other by drunkenness and brutality. The institutional church often resisted their earnest pleas; and they turned to unlikely fields in which God was pleased to bring forth returns of thirty, sixty, and one hundredfold.

So it was, too, for missionaries to American soil and for former slaves who labored among free blacks and runaway slaves. Who could have guessed then that God would find an abundant harvest in such soil? God's working has no limit if only people are willing to *hear* and to *accept*.

A Message to ■ Those Who Sow

What message from Jesus do you think is intended especially for you? Do you ever try to "hide in the crowd" to avoid having to hear your own message? If so, what has been the effect of the avoidance? of listening?

A Message to Those Who Sow

When we read a parable, we should always try to see the particular setting in which the parable is given. Sometimes no information is given. But when such information is given, we can be sure that it is important. In the case of this parable, we are told that Jesus began to teach beside the sea and that such a large crowd gathered that he got into a boat and pushed out from the shore in order to have a platform area. When the parable was finished and Jesus was alone with the disciples, they confessed that they did not understand what he had been saying. He then made clear that the parable was intended especially for them, and he went on to explain it to them.

One significant issue here is the fact of the crowd itself. The disciples must have been impressed by the growing numbers of people who were seeking Jesus. The disciples were men unaccustomed to the public eye, and now they found themselves caught up in the excitement of crowd acclaim. In a sense, they were celebrities by association, because the crowds saw them as the closest friends of the Teacher-Healer.

The disciples could hardly help but be carried away by the experience. Some of them no doubt imagined political triumphs in which they would be major figures. At just such a heady moment Jesus delivered the parable of the sower. He seemed to be saying to his disciples, "Let me tell you what the crowds are like. Let me show you how insubstantial their response is and what our ultimate goals should be."

For this is a parable for seed sowers. It is counsel for those of us who work in the fields of the Lord. And that, we must remember, is *all of us* who claim to be Christians. We are called to sow the seed of the word. And as we do so, we need to be realistic about our task.

We seem to be constantly inclined to swing from one extreme to the other. Some of us are quick to condemn ourselves when our results seem meager. Friends and perhaps even family members respond indifferently to our confession of faith. Or perhaps they join the church, then soon drop by the wayside or become preoccupied with other interests.

As a young pastor, I was saved from a good deal of self-condemnation and despair by this parable. I wanted every person who stepped inside our church to become an earnest and committed believer. Instead, I saw some come once and never again, while others joined with a show of enthusiasm, then dropped out and showed no interest in returning. Some of the best prospects became preoccupied with careers or secular projects to a point where they could only tell me that they were "just too busy."

Then one day while reading this parable I realized that Jesus had predicted just such a variety of responses. He warned us that human beings are human beings. And that includes you and me.

Working the Soil

Working the Soil

What kind of soil are you in right now?

In the course of our own life—and sometimes in the course of a single given day—we manifest the qualities of the several kinds of soil. We are sometimes hard to the point of indifference; shallow and faddish; preoccupied with cares and worries; and also, thanks be to God, fruitful and productive.

The knowledge that life's soil is so diverse should not make us complacent, but it should save us from distressing self-despair. We can remind ourselves that this is a tough game, then rise up and try again.

And through it all we must constantly

What do you think is the minimum expected of you by Jesus Christ?

The Parable and Me ■

How much seed sowing have you been doing? Are you expecting God to bring a harvest without any planting?

What can you do this week to be a good sower of the seeds of faith?

When did you last make or renew your commitment to Jesus Christ? God would welcome your prayers of commitment, and your pastor or friends in faith will be eager to support you.

Close With Prayer ■

We thank you, dear Lord, for those persons who sowed the seed of faith in our life. If it were not for their faithfulness and courage, we probably would not be in this place today. In this moment of silence, we want to thank you in the privacy of our heart for some specific persons. [A moment of silence] Now we ask that you will help us to carry on the good work so that others may experience through us what we have been privileged to receive from others. In Jesus' name we pray. **Amen.**

remind ourselves of the minimum that is expected of us: We are to go on sowing the seed of faith. If the crowds throng around us with acclaim, as they did at the moment when Jesus told the parable, we should not be too quick to congratulate ourselves. On the other hand, if all our efforts are apparently proving fruitless, we should not give in to despair. We should simply keep on sowing the seed.

Someone has said that God has not called us to be successful, but that God has called us to be faithful. It is a proper word, but to console and to correct us. We are not responsible for the condition of the soil. We *are* responsible for the spreading of the seed. The rest we shall leave to the power of the Holy Spirit.

The Parable and Me

This chapter calls us to some thoughtful self-examination. How much seed-sowing have I been doing? Am I, perhaps unconsciously, expecting God to bring a harvest without any seed being sown?

Perhaps the best seed is sown as naturally and as nearly haphazardly as that of the first-century farmer, who simply cast the seed onto the ground. We are often inclined to think of witnessing only in the context of those special occasions when we try specifically to declare our faith in Christ. But a quantity of witnessing should be present in everything we do, from being patient with a confused clerk to sending a note to a sick acquaintance. The more widely we sow the seed, the better the chance for a harvest.

This week, try consciously and constantly to be a carrier of God's word of love. Do not worry about finding a "good opportunity." Rather, sow love and faith in wonderfully reckless fashion; and see what God will do with our happy sharing.

The Father and His Two Sons
Luke 15:11-32

Session Focus ■

The most important focus of this chapter is on the love of God. Jesus portrayed that love in the story of the father. No story could say it more beautifully or persuasively than this one. Unfortunately, our familiarity with this parable may dull the message for us.

Session Objective ■

The objective of this study is to examine our attitudes, individually and collectively, toward the world's prodigals. Have we concluded that the salvation of the world's "untouchables" and "unlovables" is something best left to rescue missions or to government agencies? Or is our church's mission objective aimed precisely toward the lost?

Session Preparation ■

Think about the religious organizations in your community. Which of them, if any, are deeply involved in reaching those who are farthest away from typical church membership? Be prepared to discuss this

Some literary critics say that the parable of the prodigal son is the most beautiful story that was ever written. In only a few hundred words, it conveys pictures of youthful indifference, fatherly love, crude misuse of life, and bitter sibling rivalry. We watch a young man treat his father thoughtlessly, then come to his senses under the most painful of circumstances. Later we see the older brother being equally insensitive to his father. But through the whole story, one fact is unchanging: the love of the father.

Beautiful as this story is, however, it is also a sharp and challenging indictment of a group of religious leaders. Ironically, we lose the latter major message from the parable because we become so absorbed in the earlier message. In this study, we shall attempt to take in the whole story. For in truth, this is not only the parable of the prodigal son but also the story of a father and his two sons—both of whom, in their own ways, were prodigals. And the older brother is ultimately the focal point of the story.

God's Lost and Found

This story is one of three that come to us in the fifteenth chapter of Luke's Gospel. All three are on the same basic theme: God's question with your group members and to invite them to face the issue with you.

This chapter calls for candid, in-depth heart-searching. The subject matter prompts us to get below the surface and to see how we may have been allowing our religion to shut out others. The discussion should be carried on in a supportive, nonthreatening, but honest fashion.

Session Outline ■

Choose from among these activities and discussion starters:

God's Lost ■ and Found

Have you ever lost or misplaced something valuable and gone to a lost and found department to try to retrieve it? If so, what was your expectation? How might those expectations color your expectations of God's recovery of the lost?

Review Luke 15:3-10 as a backdrop to today's session. What are the common elements in these two parables?

concern for the lost. And all are in reply to murmuring that Jesus heard among the professional religious leaders who were critical of him. In my childhood I heard a preacher describe the fifteenth chapter of Luke as "God's Lost and Found Department," and I think I still like that description better than any other.

Luke makes clear from the outset why Jesus told these three stories. They came out of an occasion when some tax collectors and sinners were hovering near Jesus, wanting to hear him. Some of the Pharisees and scribes, who were earnestly and sometimes pretentiously religious, were offended that Jesus seemed to cater to such outcasts. The personal religious code of these Pharisees and scribes prompted them to avoid such persons. The Pharisees and scribes felt that they would be contaminated if they associated with tax collectors and the like.

So "the Pharisees and the scribes were grumbling and saying, 'This fellow welcomes sinners and eats with them' " (Luke 15:2). In response to their criticism, Jesus told three parables. The first is the story of a shepherd who finds he has lost one of his sheep and then leaves the ninety-nine other sheep in the wilderness until he can find the one that is lost. When he finds the lost sheep, he calls together friends and neighbors and asks them to rejoice with him. This parable is one of the loveliest in the Bible and has inspired many paintings and musical compositions.

The second story concerns a woman who loses a coin. She has nine others, but she is desperate for the piece that is lost. So she lights up her house and sweeps it thoroughly until she locates the coin. When she does, she too calls in friends and neighbors to celebrate her joy in recovering something missing.

The Story of the Prodigal Son ■

Read carefully Luke 15:11-32. Have on hand a commentary on Luke for added information.

What did it mean for the son to ask for his inheritance?

How does the father respond?

In terms of Jewish law, what happened to this portion of the father's estate and holdings?

What does the younger son do? In what ways might his behavior be described today?

What might be a modern interpretation of going "to a distant country"?

The Story of the Prodigal Son

And then comes the story of a father and his two sons.

One day the younger son asks his father for his share of the family estate. This is an insensitive request, for it represents an exploiting of the father and a step toward breaking the relationship between son and father. In fact, the son might have received his share at marriage (which is not indicated here), but much more likely when it was actually an inheritance. To ask for and receive this property early was to act as if his father were already dead. In addition, since the father did not assign the property to be given after his death, the son may do with it what he pleases, when under the law the father might have been protected from what we know happens next. Nevertheless, the father willingly grants the request and divides his estate between the sons.

Notice that each boy gets his share. In the laws of that time and place, this meant that the older brother got two-thirds of the property and the younger son one-third. Much of the wealth in Palestine would have been in herds and in real estate rather than in money. When we think of receiving our inheritance, we usually contemplate it in terms of cash. Apparently the son was able to convert his share to spendable goods. A significant portion of the father's wealth is now gone.

Shortly afterward the younger son leaves home. We have a feeling that this was his wish all along; he wanted to head off to the city with his money and live his own kind of life. Unfortunately, his new life is not a good one. Jesus describes his location as "a distant country," and this phrase can be seen as describing the son's spiritual journey in geographical terms. He was going into a way of life wholly different from what he had known in his father's house. We might also conjecture that in its original context, it meant heading off toward the Gentiles, yet another nail in the spiritual coffin.

There, Jesus tells us, "he squandered his property in dissolute living" (15:13). One can imagine all that is suggested in those few words. Soon the young man had spent everything. Then, just when he was destitute, famine came to the land; and none of his new friends was in a position to help him, even if they wanted to.

At last the young man found employment; but it was of the lowest kind, or at least so it seemed to Jesus' Jewish audience. For the young man got a job feeding swine. Most farmers know that this was entirely honorable work, but feeding swine did not seem so honorable to a people who considered swine religiously unclean and unfit for eating. And yet even this humble job was not the end of the disastrous circumstances. Jesus tells us that the young man was so poverty-stricken that he would gladly have eaten the pods the swine were eating, but no one gave him anything. He was helpless—and hopeless.

Repenting of the Past

At that point, Jesus said, the prodigal son "came to himself." That little phrase is a major insight into human psychology. We human beings have the ability to stand off at a distance and look at ourselves. We are apparently unlike any other creature in this respect. We can see what we could be or ought to be, and something in us can be disturbed at the distance between what we are and what we could be. That ability for self-evaluation is itself a gift of grace.

So the young man talked to himself. He

What is the significance of the young man working with pigs? How might we describe this today?

Repenting of the Past ■

How does the unique human capacity for self-reflection come to the younger son's aid? When have you "come to yourself" on an important or crucial issue? What were the results practically and faithfully?

Do you see the young man's decision to return home as courageous? desperate? selfish? some other way? Why?

What is the role of repentance in today's society? in politics? in business? in school? at church? in relationships? in your life?

A Compassionate Father

Look up "slavery" in a Bible dictionary and review Luke 15:21-24. What is the significance of the father's gifts?

Have you ever been a returned prodigal? If so, what happened when you "came to yourself"? If you did not "go back to your father," what has been the result?

The Unhappy Older Brother

How would you describe the older brother and his reaction to the younger man's return?

reminded himself that many of his father's hired hands had bread enough and to spare, even though he was starving. Then he made a grand decision: "I will get up and go to my father, and I will say to him, 'Father, I have sinned against heaven and before you; I am no longer worthy to be called your son; treat me like one of your hired hands' " (15:18-19).

So the young man set out on the journey home. While the emphasis at the beginning of the story is on traveling to "a distant country," we are not given the idea of distance when the son heads homeward. Spiritually, he made the biggest step of the journey when he "came to himself."

A Compassionate Father

One cannot miss the poignancy of the phrase "while he was still far off, his father saw him" (15:20). In those words we see a father who had long been looking for his son. In compassion, the father runs to the boy, embraces him, and kisses him. And when the young man starts to confess his sin and to explain that he wants only to be a servant in his father's house, he is lovingly interrupted. The father instructs the servants to bring the finest clothes and jewelry and to begin preparing for a party. "Get the fatted calf," he shouts, "let us eat and celebrate." Every element in the scene is one of rejoicing: a new robe; sandals (only slaves went barefoot); and a ring, the symbol of sonship.

The Unhappy Older Brother

But the mood of rejoicing ends with the appearance of the older brother. He "was in the field," for he was industrious and ambitious. As this older brother drew near the house, he heard the sounds of celebration. Instead of going in and seeing for himself, he called a servant for a report. The servant explained that his brother had returned and that the father was celebrating with a fatted calf because the boy was home safe and sound.

And now, the sad sentence in a happy story: "Then he became angry and refused to go in" (15:28). The father who had run down the road earlier in the day to welcome the younger son now goes out into the yard to appeal to the older one.

But the older brother is adamant and angry. His feelings are a mix of self-righteousness and hurt feelings. He reminds his father that he has stayed at home and served for "all these years," never disobeying his father's commands. Yet his father never gave him provisions for a party with his friends. "But when this son of yours came back"— there is a distancing of relationship here, for the servant had referred a moment before to the boy as "your brother"; the older son does not care to accept the relationship.

"This son of yours . . . has devoured your property with prostitutes" (15:30). The older brother's description of the younger son's activity may have been correct, but note that this is the first time such detail comes into the story. We are left to wonder if the older son is speaking from knowledge or just from angry suspicion. Indeed, he may even be speaking from envy; sometimes we condemn in others sins that we wish to commit ourselves.

The father is as patiently loving as ever. He reasons with the son, but we can hear the tears behind the words. "Son, you are always with me, and all that is mine is yours. But we had to celebrate and rejoice, because this brother of yours was dead, and has come back to life; he was lost and has been found" (15:31-32).

The older brother accuses the younger one of "devouring your property *with prostitutes* [italics added]." How did he know, do you think? Just a lucky guess? a wrong guess? letters from his little brother? the younger brother's poor reputation while he was still at home? What does this accusation tell us about the older brother and, therefore, about ourselves when we act similarly?

Are you secretly (or not so secretly) the "elder brother" to someone? Do you think his or her resentment is justified? Why or why not? In what measure are we personally and as church members like the elder brother?

How do we slip so unconsciously into a posture of self-righteousness? How can we protect our souls from this grievous failing?

What Does It All Mean? ■

What, to you, is the main point of the parable?

Who is the main audience?

Work in pairs to write an end to the story or to brainstorm a list of possible conclusions. How might the behaviors of each character affect him in the future? How does the new conclusion affect the point of the original story?

What effects might each conclusion have on the relationship of the characters to each other? What does this mean for you and your relationships?

The older brother had no reason why he should not also have a party; all the father's resources were there for his enjoyment whenever he might choose to use them. The father reminds him that this is your "brother," where the older boy wanted to classify him only as your "son." And then, especially, the father reminds the older son of the miracle that has taken place, the resurrection of life that occurs when someone returns from sin to a new life in the father's house.

And that is where the story ends. It does not end where our sermons and much of the artwork do, with a scene of glad reunion between the two sons. Nor does it end, as I wish it might have, with the older son joining the party.

What Does It All Mean?

To use the language of revival services, the story ends with an altar call without our ever knowing if anyone accepted the invitation. For when we go back to the beginning of the chapter, back to where the three parables are introduced, we realize to whom the stories are directed. Jesus' primary audience is not all those recognizable sinners but those scribes and Pharisees who were so unhappy that Jesus "welcomes sinners and eats with them." Those scribes and Pharisees could not help but know that they were depicted as the elder brother; for like him, they were unhappy that prodigals were being welcomed.

In all three parables Jesus' message was the same: When the lost is found, we ought to celebrate. Instead, like the older brother, these scribes and Pharisees were standing angrily outside, refusing to join the party. But we are never told how they responded to Jesus' appeal. We do not know if his parable succeeded in its purpose.

The parable offers many insights. One that is easily overlooked concerns a penalty. Because the story has such an upbeat quality in the homecoming party, we are likely to forget that sin has nevertheless taken its toll. The younger son's sins of the flesh cost him his money and reduced him to both economic and social poverty. Further, he eventually comes to see what he has done to his father. As long as he lives, he will have in his heart a memory of the pain he caused his father. Indeed, the very joy the father showed at the son's return will always be a bittersweet memory because it will forever remind him of the degree of pain his conduct caused his father.

And then, too, the younger son's body no doubt paid a price. The lifestyle he apparently followed was sure to take an eventual toll on his health. Someone has said that God forgives always, people sometimes, but nature never. Even after our sins are forgiven, we are likely to pay a continuing debt to biological laws.

As for the older brother, his sin shut out a relationship with his brother and also with his father. More than that, his sin robbed him of life's joy; he did not get in on the party.

The Grace of God

The Grace of God ■

What is the grace of God?

How would you describe the way grace is shown in this parable? To whom and by whom is it demonstrated? Is anyone left out of the opportunity for grace?

The good news of this parable is its portrayal of the grace of God. Grace is illustrated first in the younger son's experience in the generous way life itself endowed him with the blessings of a comfortable home and an indulgent father. Such good fortune is an example of what some theologians call "common grace," the favors that come to the human race even before the gift of salvation. Grace again came into the young man's life in dramatic form in the pig pen, when he "came to himself." An awakening of this sort acknowledges that God's grace goes before us; that is, grace comes to us to draw us to God even before we are inclined to see the favor of God's undeserved merit.

Grace was at its best in the waiting, forgiving father. The father was looking for his son's return and accepted him right in the midst of his statements of repentance. The father did not seek repayment from his son, nor did he demand proof that the son would never fail him again. Instead, the father called out the song of celebration, not because the son deserved it, but simply because he was thrilled to have the son back home. This is the kind of grace each of us experiences when we give our life to God.

When have you been shown lifesaving grace? What has been the result?

The homecoming party was also an act of grace. The older son was right in suggesting that he deserved a party more than his brother did. After all, we usually have parties to celebrate achievements, such as graduations, birthdays, anniversaries, or promotions. On the surface of it, this younger son merited anything but a party. He had come home in defeat, as an all-out loser. The party was an act of grace. In our more humble moments, many of us will confess that heaven will be such a party for us.

God's Patient Love

God's Patient Love ■

Have you made or renewed your commitment to Jesus Christ? If you wish, pray for God's grace to do so.

Hardly any story in the Bible is more effective in telling us of God's love for our human race. John 3:16 proclaims that God so loved the world that God gave the Son for our salvation, but this parable dramatizes that verse by showing the extremes of the reach of God's love. At first we are filled with awe that God (in the image of the father) can be so unreserved in his welcome to the son who has abused his father's love while wandering in a far country. Then later we see another expression of that love in the father's patience with a rather self-righteous older brother. The story shows God's concern for both the down-and-outer and the up-and-outer. In truth, the one needs love as badly as the other.

But the painful element of this parable is to see how sadly this love of God contrasts with the narrow-mindedness of many of us who call ourselves God's people. Those scribes and Pharisees were the most upright people in town in Jesus' day. They were earnestly and vigorously religious. They tithed, they fasted, and they fulfilled the minute details of the Mosaic law.

Nevertheless, these rigid moralists did not seem to have the remotest understanding of the heart of God. The tragedy of the older brother is that he could live a lifetime in his father's house and take in so little of his father's spirit. Unfortunately, the same thing is sometimes true of us.

Extending Grace to Others

Somehow, in the process of pursuing goodness, we can so easily be sidetracked by self-righteousness. We seem to forget that we have been received by grace and that the same grace ought to be extended to others. And the problem is accentuated if the other person's weaknesses are different from our own. We find it easier to be sympathetic with others if their sins are in some measure similar to ours.

Nor was Jesus going to be satisfied simply with tolerance for others. He was calling on all the scribes and Pharisees to rejoice in the homecoming of tax collectors and sinners. A party spirit was to prevail. Much of the relig-

Who might be a contemporary example of the scribes and Pharisees today?

Explore the comment, "The tragedy of the older brother . . ." Do you live in God's house? How well have you taken in God's Spirit?

Extending Grace to Others
When have you offered life-saving grace to another person or group of persons? What has been the result?

ion of the time did not seem to include much of the quality of gladness even in the midst of proper behavior, so introducing joy on behalf of sinners was an especially difficult task. The idea was not that sinners should be admitted somewhat grudgingly; a celebration was to be mounted in their honor!

Do you think the church can be intolerant and exclusivistic by being "nice"? How would you describe that activity?

The problem of intolerance is with us still. Churches can so easily become exclusive clubs for "nice" people. Pastors sometimes measure the quality of a group of new members on the basis of the size of their pledges or the leadership ability they will be able to offer. God's measure, if we read the New Testament correctly, is in the extent of the person's need. If the person joining our fellowship is reclaimed from abject lostness, heaven overflows with joy! That is the way Jesus expressed it to the religious people of his day, and it is a word we need to hear again.

What is your church's "vision of rejoicing over true salvation"?

Church history shows that we lose that vision of rejoicing over true salvation without knowing we have done so. Reformer Martin Luther eventually broke with the Roman Catholic Church, although his original intent was to engage in dialogue within the church about abuses he felt needed to be corrected. Over the next two centuries and later, Protestant groups grew and splintered over issues of doctrine and practice. John and Charles Wesley built the early Methodist movement from elements of society that many of their colleagues in the Anglican Church chose to ignore. But a century later, William Booth left the British Methodist movement to start the Salvation Army after Methodism seemed to reject his concern for the slum dwellers of England's great cities. Becoming "respectable," or perhaps too comfortable, is an inviting tendency. We may

The Parable and Me

Review and answer the questions in the first two paragraphs here.

This parable and the two that precede it in Luke 15 all emphasize the mood of celebration. "Rejoice with me" is the recurring theme. To what degree are our churches marked by such a spirit? What can we do in both worship services and on social occasions to give our churches more of a feeling that calls out, "Rejoice with me"?

Close With Prayer

Receive prayer requests at the end of the session; they should be both general and specifically related to the issues of the lesson. Then close with this prayer:

We gladly acknowledge that the prodigal's father is you, O God, and that we also are your children. We thank you for the grace we have received in our lives. Forgive us, we pray, that we have not always realized the extent of your mercy and have not been as grateful as we ought to have been. And help us, loving Lord, to extend to others the kindness we have received. Make us instruments of your grace, so that some younger or elder brother may feel the glad embrace of your divine heart. With thankful and joyful hearts we pray, and in Jesus' name. Amen.

become so respectable, in fact, that we may not have room for a heavenly Father who cares profoundly for a lost creation.

The Parable and Me

This session calls for earnest soul searching. How willing am I to receive into the fellowship of the church people who are fresh from the swine pens of life? Do I rejoice as much when our church brings in a marginal teenager or an unstable adult as I do when the new member is a leading person in the community? Do I pledge to support our church's clothes closet and hunger program but ask a dirty street person who needs help to wait outside until the church service is over?

And do I seek out such tax collectors and sinners for Christ and for my church? Or do I become uneasy at the thought of going after such people, wondering how my fellow members will react to their presence?

Perhaps the best way to put the lesson of this parable into practice is to ask God to give us a clearer vision of those who need love desperately. Then begin seeking ways as an individual to reach out to such persons, and think of ways your congregation might do so. The measure of need is not simply or always economic poverty. Some of the greatest times of need occur when we are financially secure and socially esteemed.

The Mustard Seed
Matthew 13:31-32

Session Focus ■

Nearly everyone who comes to a study class is (or has been) a church member. This lesson should encourage two points of emphasis. First, the church is of God. Second, let us ask ourselves what kind of persons we ought to be if we are part of an organization that claims to be God's body on earth. This is a quite astonishing concept if we dare to take it seriously.

Session Objective ■

This session should increase our faith in God's purposes in the world, and it should deepen our personal dedication to our part in fulfilling these purposes.

Session Preparation ■

Pray for your own renewed feeling of excitement about God's kingdom and the human instrumentalities through which God works. Consider getting out a hymnal and reading the words of some of the great hymns that are found under such headings as "The kingdom of God" or "The mission of the

Probably the greatest problem we face in studying this parable is that we know so little about it—and worse, that perhaps we care even less. That is, *kingdom of heaven* is not a term that seems related to our lives in any tangible way. That makes it difficult for us to get excited about a story that talks about the kingdom of heaven and a mustard seed.

In one sense, it is surprising that the kingdom of heaven does not interest us more. After all, each time we say the Lord's Prayer, we repeat the phrase, "Thy kingdom come." In that sense, the term is one of the most common in our liturgical language. But obviously we do not think about what we are saying when we pray for God's kingdom to come. If we did, the kingdom of heaven would interest us more.

And surely it ought to when we consider its prominence in the ministry of Jesus. We are inclined to think that Jesus' message centered on mercy, healing, and advice for daily living; but Matthew tells us that as Jesus began to teach, it was with the message, "Repent, for the kingdom of heaven has come near" (Matthew 4:17)—the same theme John the Baptist had used as he prepared the way for Jesus (Matthew 3:2). As Jesus went throughout Galilee teaching, it was with "the good news of the kingdom" (Matthew 4:23). Even the Beatitudes begin church." See how hopeful our ancestors have been, and take hope with them.

Session Outline ■

Choose from among these activities and discussion starters:

The Kingdom of God ■

What is your initial idea of what the kingdom of God is? (You will look at this more later.)

Review these passages in Matthew, using a commentary for further reference.

Write down the key phrases from the Lord's Prayer: "Your kingdom come, Your will be done, on earth as it is in heaven" where they can be seen by all. What does the Lord's Prayer tell you about the Kingdom?

with a reference to the kingdom: "Blessed are the poor in spirit, for theirs is the kingdom of heaven" (Matthew 5:3).

The Kingdom of God

Basically, the kingdom of God or the kingdom of heaven means *God's sovereign reign and rule*. But Jesus used the term in several different ways, which can easily prove confusing to us. As we have already noticed, he told the people that the kingdom had "come near"; but then he said that the poor in spirit already possessed it. He warned the people that unless their righteousness exceeded that of the scribes and Pharisees, they would "never enter the kingdom of heaven" (Matthew 5:20). He explained to his disciples that the greatest in the kingdom would have to become as humble as a child (Matthew 18:1-4). No doubt, it is because Jesus spoke so much about the Kingdom that his disciples expected him to set up an earthly empire where they could be his chief assistants, at his right hand and at his left.

I think we can rightly say several things about the kingdom of God. For one, it is God's ultimate goal for our lives and for our world; thus it is that we pray,

Your kingdom come,
Your will be done,
    on earth as it is in heaven.
            (Matthew 6:10)

This prayer also defines the kingdom of God in the most practical terms: It is where God's will is done. But, of course, you may well reply that although that is a practical definition, it is also an imprecise one. After all, it may be presumptuous of us to say when God's will is being done. We believe, then, that the Kingdom is a future goal but that it is also a present and living reality. We are both the participants in and the recipients of the blessings of the Kingdom.

Building the ■ Kingdom

When, do you think, does the Kingdom come? How does it come?

Building the Kingdom

I think it can fairly be said that the kingdom of God comes in our own individual lives whenever, and to whatever degree, we submit to the will of God. Each of us is a little kingdom of God, a land where God desires to be in control. But it is also true, it seems to me, that God's kingdom is meant to extend to all humankind; that is why we pray for God's kingdom to come "on earth as it is in heaven."

When I was a young preacher, great Christian reformers still spoke passionately about "building the kingdom of God." It was a large theme that included such matters as an end to gambling, opposition to the liquor traffic, world peace, and an end to racial and ethnic prejudice. Some of the theological thinking behind these movements may have been flawed; but the reformer in me—and the idealist too—still tingles at such hymn lines as, "O Zion, haste, thy mission high fulfilling" and "Save us from weak resignation to the evils we deplore." Much as I believe in personal conversion, I am uneasy with worship that too easily turns inward to our own blessing and that is not stirred to march against the world's need and pain. It is not enough that the kingdom of God is at work within me; I also want for God's kingdom to come on earth.

Are there any great battles currently raging on behalf of the Kingdom? If so, what are they? Are you participating in the fray? Why or why not?

The Kingdom of ■
Heaven Is Like...
Using a commentary on Matthew, look up and review quickly these other parables of the Kingdom.

The Kingdom of Heaven Is Like . . .

The thirteenth chapter of Matthew's Gospel is made up almost entirely of parables, and they are all parables of the kingdom of heaven. The first is about the word of the kingdom (13:1-23), followed by the parable of the weeds among the wheat (13:24-30, 36-43). That busy sower who had just planted seed in many different soils sowed good wheat seeds in a fertile field. But an enemy planted weeds among the wheat. Both grew together until the harvest, when the good plants were separated from the bad.

Next, after the mustard seed, is the comparison to yeast (13:33), then to hidden treasure (13:44), to a buried pearl (13:45-46), and to a huge catch of all kinds of fish (13:47-50). These stories or comparisons have some elements in common.

First, the sower, the wheat and weeds, and the catch of fish indicate the sad human truth that not everything turns out as we would like. The good and the bad, the loyal and the disloyal, the fruitful and the unproductive, exist side by side. One way or another, God will sort it out in God's eternal kingdom.

What are the common identifiers of the Kingdom? What do they mean to you now?

Second, the Kingdom is like something hidden (yeast), perhaps buried away (the pearl and treasure), that is so intrinsically valuable one would sacrifice all to have it once one realized that it exists.

The Parable of ■
the Mustard Seed
Read Matthew 13:31-32. Use a Bible dictionary or commentary to gain extra information on the image of the seed.

The Parable of the Mustard Seed

The parable of the mustard seed (13:31-32) is brief, hardly more than a dramatized figure of speech. "The kingdom of heaven," Jesus says, "is like a mustard seed that someone took and sowed in his field" (13:31). Then Jesus tells us two or three things about this seed: It is "the smallest of all the seeds";

How might the disciples and other early followers of Jesus have understood this parable?

If the mustard seed/shrub image seems foreign to you, what image might you substitute?

but when it reaches its fullness, "it is the greatest of shrubs," almost like a tree, in fact, "so that the birds of the air come and make nests in its branches" (13:32).

Obviously the point of this parable is the wonder of something so small becoming important all out of proportion to its original size. This parable must have been tremendously encouraging to Jesus' disciples. For no matter how they may have been excited by the mounting crowds and by the miracles Jesus was working, they could not help but see that the power structures of society lay elsewhere—with the Roman government in matters of politics and with the scribes and Pharisees in issues of religion.

In their realistic moments the disciples had to feel a bit uneasy as they looked over their own number. They were small business people, at best. They were running one-person operations or were part of family businesses, and usually fishing businesses at that. So when Jesus said that the kingdom of heaven is like something that is next to nothing but that develops until it supports a host of others, the disciples must have squared their shoulders and smiled with new confidence.

I do not think there are many hidden messages in this simple parable. Jesus referred to the mustard seed as "the smallest of all the seeds," not because it was literally so (in fact, some seeds were even smaller), but because this was a common phrase in the time and place Jesus spoke.

How does exaggeration (smallest seed/greatest shrub) enhance or complicate your understanding of the parable?

The mustard seed was proverbial for its smallness; it was used often as a figure of speech to describe something minute. And, of course, Jesus' hearers were familiar with the astonishing growth of this plant. Visitors to the Middle East report seeing mustard plants that reach ten or twelve feet in height. And because its seeds are so attractive to birds, the birds of the air come in veritable clouds to settle on the branches.

Thus when Jesus used the term, all of his listeners tuned in appreciatively. The Gospel of Mark tells us, again by exaggerating, that the seed grows into the greatest of all shrubs; Luke says it is a tree. As a shrub or small tree, it is hardly the most majestic of all plants; but then, the disciples were not the most majestic of all human beings either. Nevertheless, they were to accomplish greater things than they could ever have imagined.

Look at John 14:12. Does the parable of the mustard seed give deeper meaning to the John passage? If so, what new understanding do you gain?

Perhaps if Jesus were teaching in our day, he might say that the kingdom of heaven is like the genetic code— small almost beyond measure, but hidden within it is the whole physical makeup of a human being. Still and all, the mustard seed tells the story better, even if not quite so dramatically, because people from primitive bush country to the urban apartment dweller who grows spices in a rooftop garden can catch the wonder of growth that the mustard seed represents.

The Importance of Small Beginnings ■

Is there any motto, slogan, book or song title, or other saying that carries meaning for you similar to "Little Is Much When God Is in It"? If so, what is it? What has it meant to you?

The Importance of Small Beginnings

When I was a boy, my parents had a small book—hardly more than an extended pamphlet—that was titled "Little Is Much When God Is in It." I cannot reconstruct the story, though I remember that it was a lovely record of a humble person's simple deed that had a series of extended results, like the widening reach of circles. But the title has always remained with me because I believe so strongly in the principle.

All of us have opportunities to do little things; we never can guess how far reaching some of the results may be. The book emphasized that the secret of such influence was in God's involvement. The same principle is at work in Jesus' parable. There is a tree of potential in every mustard seed of Christian effort.

William Barclay, the popular Bible expositor, illustrates the point with a story from English history. William Wilberforce had read an exposure of the slave trade by Thomas Clarkson. Some time later he was sitting one afternoon with George Grenville and Great Britain's great Prime Minister Pitt in Pitt's garden at Holwood. In that setting, Wilberforce was pondering the unseemly ugliness of slavery when suddenly Pitt turned to him and asked, "Wilberforce, why don't you give a notice of a motion on the slave trade?" That seed planted in Wilberforce's mind began the death knell for the slave trade in England.

Many of us can recall some occasion when a single sentence or a brief conversation changed our lives. It may have been a teacher who encouraged us to believe in our potential or a parent who insisted on integrity at a crucial moment. Some of us would agree with the mangled sentence of the great baseball manager Casey Stengel, who said, "There comes a time in every man's life, and I've had many of them." We can recall, not only one life-directing sentence or conversation, but numbers of them. And we are grateful for every one.

God seems to be on the side of small things. We recall the instance in Israel's history when their nation was at war with their traditional enemy, the Philistines. Young Jonathan, son of King Saul, found himself near the Philistine garrison with only his armor bearer. He looked upon the uneven odds as an opportunity. "It may be that the

What is the most transformational or life-changing moment you can recall? What happened? What has been the result? Do you think God had a hand in it? Explain your answer.

What examples do you know of "bigger is better" or of "smaller is better"?

In what ways have you seen God to be on the side of small things?

LORD will act for us," he said to his aide, "for nothing can hinder the LORD from saving by many or by few" (1 Samuel 14:6).

It may even be that we hold greater potential for God when our resources are small because our limitations cause us to rely more fully on God's power. When we are unduly self-confident, we trust in ourselves rather than in God. Then, too, when we have more, we tend often to be more conservative; we are cautious because we have so much to lose! But when our resources are small, we grow more willing to risk; and that willingness becomes a setting where faith can work.

Do you believe that having great resources discourages us from reliance on God? If so, is this true for you?

The Church Began Small . . .

Most of us are inclined to think of the church as the kingdom of God on earth—not any particular denomination, of course, but the whole body of Christian believers. This is the full meaning of the "kingdom of God," but the church is surely a key factor in the kingdom of heaven.

The believers together, Paul told us, are the body of Christ—each member with greater or lesser abilities, but nevertheless mutually interdependent. When the head and hand and foot and eye are the best heads, hands, feet, and eyes they can be, the church, the Kingdom on earth, grows into the body that gives honor to God.

The growth of the church certainly fits the mustard seed theme. One cannot imagine a less auspicious beginning than what we have in the church. At first there were only twelve rather average men, and one of them defected. Others, including a number of loyal women, were in the second circle of followers; so after the Resurrection there were roughly 120 who were waiting for the Holy Spirit at Pentecost. We have no reason to

The Church Began Small . . .

What does it mean that the church is the body of Christ? (See also 1 Corinthians 12:12-31.)

With what part of the body do you associate yourself? Why?

In what ways was this first body of Christ (and later ones as well) plagued with thick head, fumbling hands, and so on?

think that the group included any notable leaders. These people were often enough characterized by thick heads, fumbling hands, clumsy feet, and blind eyes.

They took as their symbol their leader's disgrace, his execution by crucifixion, and set out to tell the world that he had been raised from the dead. For generations this growing band of Christians was intermittently persecuted and driven underground. Nevertheless, they grew so steadily and so rapidly that before long they were in every part of the Roman Empire and probably far beyond.

. . .and Grew to Be Great ■

■ . . . and Grew to Be Great

Their history has been uneven. At times, they have conducted themselves in ways utterly unlike the standards of Jesus, their leader. Sometimes they have seemed more like the evil they oppose than like the Savior they profess to follow. Yet with all that, they are today the largest religious body in the world. Christian believers are literally in every part of the world; and in those isolated places where we have not yet made a witness, we claim the commitment to take a stand as soon as possible. As a result, our strange symbol, the cross, is the most widely recognized symbol of any kind, sacred or secular, in all the earth. Talk about a mustard seed becoming a plant! The figure of speech is almost modest compared to what has happened.

The sentence, "The birds of the air come and make nests in its branches" (13:32) is open to several possible interpretations. Some think of it as a positive picture: the church becoming an institution of such strength that people find shelter and nourishment there.

Others see it as a negative, remembering

Who are "the birds of the air" who come to "make nests in its branches"? How do we participate in building those nests?

that the "birds of the air" are several times symbolic of evil in the Bible. These people interpret the "birds" as representing all those persons and movements who reside under the auspices of the church but who are not true to its Lord or to his teachings.

I think it is appropriate to apply this parable at a personal level too. It is not the main theme of the parable, but it is a legitimate insight. That is, God often works in our lives through small beginnings. The measure of God's kingdom that is revealed in our lives almost always begins in some modest way.

But it is clear that Jesus was seeking to describe God's larger purposes in our world. God has a dream for humankind, a kingdom of heaven. It is a setting where the will of God is done, just as it is in heaven.

Growing Pains

We seem a long way from that ideal. History suggests that each time we make two steps forward, we slip a step backward. Just when we think some particular evil is wiped out, it manifests itself in another form, like a virus that develops immunity to our best antibiotic. In the church we experience wonderful periods of spiritual renewal, but they almost never extend to a second generation; and usually we see tragic perversions even in the midst of the renewals—instances of division, self-seeking leadership, or cheap exploitation.

But just when we might be ready to give up, God raises a new banner of hope. Sometimes it is a truly good human being; at other times a movement; and yet again an almost subtle sense of awakening, like the breath of God's Holy Spirit. At such times we have to conclude that this really is God's kingdom and that the cause can never be lost when it is God's cause.

List great Christian believers, both past and present, who give evidence that God has been, and continues to be, at work in our world. What do you know of their beginnings?

Growing Pains ■

What are some of the ways the church has lost steps by apparently going backward?

What are some of the small and great steps forward that the church has accomplished?

So it is our business to throw ourselves anew into the struggle. If the odds are against us, that is nothing new; they have been against most of our ancestors in the faith. Frankly, it is hard to assess the state of the battle in our time. On the one hand, we look to Europe and note that Christianity has become, for all practical purposes, a minority so small that it is hardly more than a historical reference. On the other hand, Christianity is growing so rapidly in some parts of Africa and Asia that we cannot keep the statistics current.

What reasons do you see for the losses and gains? What can be done to eliminate losses and maximize gains? What can you do?

In the United States itself, we also have a balancing of data. The great media channels—print and video—are as secular as they have been in quite some time; indeed, one might say that they are militantly secular. Some branches of the church are losing ground statistically and apparently are not very troubled that this is so. But in other settings, Christianity is vigorous and enthusiastic.

The best thing I know is that this is God's kingdom about which we are talking. Therefore, any discussion of its future is entirely speculative because we do not know how God may choose to speak or to intervene.

Reclaiming "Kingdom"

That brings us to a term that is offensive to some—the very word *kingdom*. We are such individualists and so much the product of democracy that the term grates on some nerves. A writer whom I respect has begun substituting the word *commonwealth* for *kingdom*.

Reclaiming "Kingdom" ■

Now what image do you have of the Kingdom?

I suggest that we get comfortable with the ancient word *kingdom*, however. It is not a sexist word, though it is built on the base of "king"; but it is a word suggesting absolute authority.

And why not? God is not our presiding officer. God has not been elected to office. God is God. Indeed, we need to remember that when Jesus (and John the Baptist before him) announced the Kingdom, it was with the call that we *repent*. One does not come into the kingdom of God announcing his or her rights or negotiating for position. We enter by the humble door of repentance. And then we find ourselves in gladness and grandeur such as we could never imagine.

And it all begins with a mustard seed.

The Parable and Me

This lesson ought to encourage us to think about the church as a divinely ordained institution and then about how we ought to relate to an institution whose ultimate purposes are in God.

This is a difficult concept. Not so much intellectually; we buy the concept itself without much trouble. It is when we get down to the nitty-gritty of weekly church life that we find it hard to realize that the church belongs to God. It is not our club or our society; it is not even our reform movement.

The church, at its best, is an outpost of God's kingdom, a foreshadowing of the perfected eternal kingdom of God. The church at its worst, or its much-less-than-best, is what disappoints and discourages the faithful and gives ammunition to the unbelieving to charge it with hypocrisy and self-service. When at the extremes laity hunker down to "protect" the church from others unlike themselves or clergy abuse their office with immoral or felonious behavior or when in the name of God distorted and sick persons commit heinous crimes against others, God surely weeps over such sins against the Kingdom.

What does it mean to you to think of God as a sovereign ruler? What images seem best to describe God to you?

The Parable and Me ■

What are some of the ways the church has been its smallest? most distorted? most disappointing? What effect, if any, has this had on you?

What are some of the ways the kingdom of God on earth has seemed at its most effective? its most magnificent? What effect, if any, has this had on you?

What about the church seems most vital to you? What is your part in that vitality?

This is a good lesson for looking at the church beyond our own parish. We need to remind ourselves, at first, of its great (if mottled) history. See how we have survived, against impossible odds! We have survived not only the persecution of those who have hated us but also the embrace of those who have loved us poorly or selfishly.

Then we need to see the wider reach of the church in our own day. If we are part of a congregation that is struggling to survive, we may find it hard to imagine the vitality the church enjoys in many parts of the world and in many places in our own particular countries. We ought, especially, to celebrate those great souls both past and present who prove the wonder of the Christian gospel by the beauty and integrity of their lives. It is an honor to be associated with such magnificent souls and a sacred memory as well.

Now what seems to be the main point, for you, of the parable of the mustard seed?

If you wish, take this time to make or renew a commitment to God as a member of the body of Christ and as a vital part of the Kingdom.

Close With Prayer ■

Close the class session with this prayer:

Lord of all little things, forgive our fascination with bigness. You chose to enter our earth as a child; that should be proof enough that you are not as taken with size as we are. Remembering that, we may hold our breath in anticipation each time we see something small, something unlikely, something divinely wonderful. Help us to see that you are at work in even our humblest enterprises. In Jesus' name we pray. Amen.

The Good Samaritan
Luke 10:25-37

Can anything good come out of an argument? Not often, probably. But there are no limits to the instruments God can use to teach us and to transform us, and even arguments can sometimes serve a purpose.

The parable under discussion in this chapter was stimulated by an argumentative man. The Gospel writer tells us as much in the sentence that introduces the parable: "Just then a lawyer stood up to test Jesus" (Luke 10:25). On the surface the lawyer asks a question as if he were a seeker after faith. But Luke has warned us that the lawyer has a hidden agenda, and that agenda is revealed without much delay.

A Surface Interest in Religion

Apparently the lawyer of our story is a man who wants to keep God safely at arm's length. He is neither the first nor the last person to have used religion as a buffer between himself and God. The word *religion* comes from a Latin root meaning "to bind back together," but all of us know that sometimes we use religion to hold God or others at a distance. So it was with the first-century lawyer.

We should note at the outset that a lawyer in the Jewish tradition of the first century was also a theologian. After all, the only law the Jews knew (other than the law that was lenge participants to suggest ways to be "good Samaritans." Emphasize the idea of neighbors both near and far.

Session Outline ■

Choose from among these activities and discussion starters:

A Surface Interest ■ in Religion

What does religion mean to you? What, do you think, is the aim of religion? the purpose?

Who were the scribes, lawyers, and religious teachers of Jesus' day? (Use a Bible dictionary if you need to.) How are they alike or different from their counterparts today?

Read Leviticus 19:8 and Deuteronomy 6:4-9. What do those passages mean? What do they mean to you?

forced upon them by a foreign power like the Romans) was the law of Moses and those interpretations that had grown around it. So a lawyer was not so much a civil authority, as in modern society, but a religious one.

This context explains why the lawyer brought to Jesus a question that you and I would consider to be profoundly religious. "Teacher, . . . what must I do to inherit eternal life?" (10:25). He was a lawyer; and he expected to find the answer to this question in the books of the Law, the teachings of Moses.

Jesus referred the lawyer back to his own sources. This was a skillful teaching strategy on Jesus' part, for we understand best when we dig out the answers for ourselves. "What is written in the law?" Jesus asked. "What do you read there?"

The lawyer showed that he was a perceptive student. He went right past all the peripheral matters and picked out two key commandments from the Hebrew Scriptures. "You shall love the Lord your God with all your heart, and with all your soul, and with all your strength, and with all your mind; and your neighbor as yourself" (10:27). With this answer the lawyer brought together a passage from Leviticus 19:8 and one from the Shema, Deuteronomy 6:5, two units of Scripture that every Jew knew by heart.

The lawyer's answer could not be improved upon, and Jesus praised him for it. "You have given the right answer; do this, and you will live" (Luke 10:28). But, of course, there is a big leap from an answer in theory and the application of that answer in the specifics of everyday living. The lawyer knew as much, and he wanted to be clear as to what those specifics might be.

Trying to Measure Love ■

When have you heard the truth (though not to your liking) and tried to "justify" yourself? Did you succeed? If so, what was the result? What was the lawyer trying to do?

How might the law in this instance have been a trap rather than a blessing? Do you ever try to get around the spirit of the law by adhering strictly to the letter of the law?

Can you measure love? Explain.

An Effective Ilustration ■

Read 2 Samuel 12. Review a Bible commentary on the passage if you can. How was David drawn into the story Nathan told? What was the result?

Trying to Measure Love

But more than that, unfortunately, the lawyer wanted "to justify himself." *Love* is such an imprecise word; it is open to interpretation, depending on the outlook of the person. On the one hand, a shallow person can easily say, "I love everybody" and give the matter no further thought. A painfully sensitive person, by contrast, might live under a sense of constant condemnation in the realization that he or she has not yet experienced certain altruistic expressions of love.

The lawyer was a practical man. He wanted a measure for love. After all, the law regarding honoring the sabbath by not working had been refined by the rabbis until it was measured in how many steps could be walked and what particular deeds could be done. Perhaps this new teacher from Nazareth could come up with an exact standard for love.

And clearly enough, the lawyer felt that whatever definition Jesus gave, the lawyer would come out looking rather good. He must have reasoned that his conduct was as good as almost anyone else's; so surely whatever Jesus' answer, he would meet its requirements.

An Effective Illustration

Jesus replied to the lawyer's inquiry with a parable. Among the stories Jesus told, few are better known. In fact, this story is so well known that the phrase "a good Samaritan" has become a phrase in our common speech, used by millions of people who have no religious persuasion or who may not even know the source of the words they use.

Life has many truths that are hard to accept if they come to us in straight, unvarnished factual form. A story can be especially effective for illustrating difficult realities and human failings.

The prophet Nathan used such a device with King David after David sinned with Bathsheba and arranged the murder of Uriah. Nathan would have received a poor hearing from David if he had simply said, "You are guilty of adultery and murder." But Nathan captured David's attention and even his sympathies when he told the story of the poor farmer who had only one ewe lamb and who was shamefully misused by his wealthy neighbor (2 Samuel 12). When at last Nathan said, "You are the man!" there was no door through which David could escape.

In the same fashion, Jesus wove a story that captured the lawyer. Undoubtedly the story also captured the attention of the people who were eavesdropping on the discussion. Many of them must have known the lawyer and probably held him in grudging respect. No doubt, many of them were eager in their own life to get Jesus' answer. They must have leaned forward in warm anticipation to see where the story would go.

When has a story that seems to be relevant only obliquely struck right at the heart of a matter for you? What happened?

The Story of the Good Samaritan

The Story of the Good Samaritan

Read Luke 10:25-37 and look it up in a Bible commentary for more information. Then retell it in your own words.

A man was traveling from Jerusalem to Jericho, and he fell among robbers. The crowd easily understood this introduction. That stretch of road was one of the most dangerous in the whole area. All along the road were lonely regions where thieves could spring out from the caves and overpower a solitary traveler. These robbers not only took all the man had, they stripped him of his clothing, then beat him until he was nearly dead. A peculiar insanity seems to take over human beings at times; once they have let their lawlessness loose, they don't know how

Who were the people who passed by without helping? What expectations might one have had regarding their level of interest in or concern for the victim? Were those expectations met? If so, why? How?

Try roleplaying the parable. Select a priest, a Levite, and a Samaritan in advance; and ask each one to make a short speech as if she or he were explaining to friends his or her actions. What excuse did they have for going by on the other side? Then the Samaritan should indicate some of the struggle within himself before he finally did his deed of mercy.

What was the relationship of the Samaritans to the Jews?

What reason did the Samaritan have for stopping to help? Was this surprising to or expected by the original hearers of the story?

to stop it. So it was in this instance that theft led to brutality.

But a hopeful sound was soon heard. A priest was traveling down the road. He represented the highest religious leadership in the land. The people in the crowd must have expected that Jesus was going to use him as an example of how a human being ought to show love to another human being. After all, what more likely example could there be? But, no doubt to the surprise of the listeners, Jesus noted that the priest, when he saw the man, passed by on the other side. Perhaps some in the crowd made excuses in their mind, reasoning that the priest was probably on his way to perform some religious function where he dared not be late or that he was afraid of being made unclean in the ceremonial law by approaching what might be a dead body.

Then, Jesus continued, a Levite came by. We could describe him as a lay associate of the priest and also a person of religious vocation. He, too, when he saw the dying man, hurried over to the other side of the road.

And then a Samaritan approached. The listeners, like the lawyer, were no doubt all Jewish. No body of people was despised as much by the Jews as were the Samaritans. Jews considered Samaritans to be inferior both racially and religiously and would go to almost any lengths to avoid association with them. Probably some in the crowd expected that this Samaritan would work still further violence on the victim; that's the sort of conduct they expected from Samaritans.

But to the crowd's surprise, Jesus portrayed the Samaritan as a heroic figure. He was apparently a person of great heart; for when he saw the poor traveler, he "was moved with pity" (Luke 10:33). Instead of

If you wish, retell the story using contemporary characters. What further insight, if any, does the retelling provide?

moving to the other side of the road, the Samaritan "went to him" and began caring for him. He bound up the victim's wounds, pouring on the items he had in his baggage, oil and wine. Then he put the man on his own beast and brought him to the nearest inn. There the Samaritan watched over the wounded man through the night. The next morning the Samaritan gave the innkeeper the equivalent of about two days' wages and said, "Take care of him; and when I come back; I will repay you whatever more you spend" (10:35).

Being a Neighbor ■

Who was the neighbor? How would you describe a good neighbor?

Being a Neighbor

By this time, no doubt, the crowd and the lawyer were in stunned silence. Now it was Jesus' turn to ask a question: "Which of these three, do you think, was a neighbor to the man who fell into the hands of the robbers?" (10:36). The lawyer was honest enough to confess the point: "The one who showed him mercy" (10:37). Jesus concluded with a call to committed action: "Go and do likewise" (10:37).

What contrast is there between the question the lawyer asked and what Jesus answered?

The first thing that strikes us about this parable is that Jesus did not directly answer the lawyer's question. He had asked, "Who is my neighbor?" The story Jesus told answered the question, "To whom can I be a neighbor?" Jesus changed "neighbor" from object to subject. Identifying my neighbor is not difficult when I am willing to be a neighbor.

How did Jesus define *neighbor*?

And in another case, Jesus defined *neighbor* in the most dramatic and painful way. Our neighbor is any human being who is in need of neighboring. The dying traveler ought to have been recognized as a neighbor by both the priest and the Levite. As a matter of fact, he was more a neighbor to them than to the Samaritan; for the beaten man was almost

In what ways did the priest and Levite succeed or fail at being a neighbor? How is their experience like yours? unlike yours?

certainly a Jew and thus a kinsman to the priest and Levite and a traditional enemy to the Samaritan.

Also, the two religious workers might well have confessed that their religion compelled them to live in a larger neighborhood than do the unreligious. After all, if God is the Creator, the whole human race is God's concern. If I am seeking to please God, the whole world must also be my concern. Unfortunately, neither clergypersons nor laypersons are always consistent in applying their theology to the circumstances of life. Clearly, the priest and Levite failed to do so.

Someone has said that good religion is also good sense. The secular world doesn't always recognize the truth of this statement because the secular view is often shortsighted. Certainly, the parable of the good Samaritan was far ahead of its time. For in this parable we learn that every human being is our potential neighbor. The Samaritan recognized that the injured man was his neighbor even though the man belonged to an ethnic group that despised him and that he no doubt despised in return.

The lesson of true neighborliness is far more significant in our day when the boundaries of our neighborhoods are so much wider. Our grandparents could limit their practice of neighborliness to a relatively small area. That is no longer possible for you and me. Modern communication and high-speed transportation have made most of the world into one giant neighborhood.

As a result, if an epidemic breaks out today in a remote area of Asia, we may well fear that the dread disease will invade our borders in a few weeks. By the same token, if an ordinary working man in one of the European nations is unhappy with his state

How has the "shrinking of the world" through mass communication affected the notion of neighbor? Does knowing about the plight of people halfway around the world connect you as a neighbor? Do you think others in the world who are aware of news in the US consider you a neighbor? If so, explain.

In what ways can we be neighbors to people outside the immediate circle of our church or our daily friendships? How can we be neighbors in any significant way to people in other parts of the world?

of life, we may one day feel the shock waves in Kalamazoo. Such is the nature of the small world in which we live. As a result, we should hear the story of the good Samaritan and the lesson it teaches with sensitivity.

This parable also teaches us that love for our neighbors helps our world grow smaller and larger at the same moment and in the same act. The world grows smaller in that we come to realize that we are all one family and that the whole great planet can be taken into our embrace. The most distant continent is in our neighborhood, barely around the corner.

But our personal world also grows *larger.* An old rhyme spoke of a small world:

What is your reaction to this little poem? Explain your reaction.

Lord, bless me and my wife,
   My son John, and his wife.
We four
   And no more.

Many people live in just such a small world. Their boundaries are limited to their kind of people, and nothing more. That makes for a painfully tiny world. The spirit of the Samaritan enlarges our world until it includes not only people who are different from us but also people in every part of the world. Where once I felt concern only for my family or my street or my circle of friends, now I find myself reaching out to the far stretches of humankind.

What Can One Individual Do? ■

What simple, near-at-hand acts make for good neighbors?

Do you think being visionary enhances, detracts

What Can One Individual Do?

How do we accomplish such grand, far-reaching purposes? By simple, near-at-hand acts. If the Samaritan had been a visionary, he might have slipped past the wounded man as easily as the priest and Levite did. He could have reasoned that little would be from, or has no effect on neighborliness? Why?

How do you or others philosophize away opportunities to be a good neighbor?

accomplished in the grand scheme of things by aiding one unknown traveler. His action would not decrease the threat of war in the world, would not relieve the oppression of the Roman government, and probably would not even improve relationships between the Jews and Samaritans. In other words, it would contribute nothing to solving the world's overwhelming problems.

But in our world of great issues, all of us have to remember that no issue is more important than the human individual. Mother Teresa became an example to us through her ability to understand this fact. She had made it her commitment to Christ to rescue newborn infants from the trash cans of teeming cities and to carry dying people from the streets. A large percentage of those she rescued died within a few days, so some people asked Mother Teresa why she bothered. She answered that a human being has a right to die in a setting of love.

What example did Mother Teresa provide as a good neighbor? What qualities or traits enabled her work?

Mother Teresa acknowledged that her work was only a drop of water in the ocean. But if she had not cared for that one drop, she argued, the ocean would be one drop less. By now the people she picked out of life's refuse heaps number into the thousands. But her work had to begin with just one person. The Samaritan kind of commitment always begins with one.

Emphasis on the individual does not minimize great causes, and it surely is not meant to suggest that we should not involve ourselves in far-reaching matters. This point only encourages each of us to do the work that is at hand. After all, who can estimate how much goodwill eventually comes from one act of kindness? We follow One who built a miracle on the loaves-and-fishes lunch of one small boy.

What was the response of the people in the crowd who heard Jesus' parable?

Sometimes the most significant neighbor of all is a member of our own family. Most of us have known someone who poured great energy into community activities or into kindnesses to other people while being neglectful of spouse, children, or parent. Discuss the importance of being a neighbor to those who are closest to us.

An Unfinished Story ■

If you have time, make up one or more alternate endings to the parable. What new insights or possibilities arise?

What do you think was the right thing to do for each character? Why?

One wonders, too, how the lawyer and the people in the crowd dealt with the fact that the hero in Jesus' story was a Samaritan. They could not simply push the matter aside because it was too sensitive an issue in their lives.

Perhaps Jesus' use of a Samaritan as the key figure caused some of them to reject the story outright. Others may have stored this fact away in the angry section of their brain, to be remembered when the multitudes began to turn against Jesus. We hope, of course, that the people were so deeply stirred by the point Jesus was making that they enlarged their definition of "neighbor" to include the despised Samaritan. Surely some did. But no doubt some of the listeners were "rocky soil" and quickly rejected the whole idea of a Samaritan being good. "That shows what a dreamer the Nazarene is," someone might have remarked, "to think that anything good could come out of Samaria."

An Unfinished Story

As in many of the parables, the story Jesus told was open ended, not really completed. We do not know if the Samaritan returned or when, if he paid the remainder of the bill, if the victim survived, if the victim was grateful to have been helped even by a dreaded Samaritan, if he would rather have remained in the ditch than be touched so intimately by a despised stranger, if the innkeeper did take care in the Samaritan's absence. New implications and new possibilities unfold as each "if" is added to the story, creating nearly endless possibilities to accept or maneuver around what was the right thing to do.

Likewise, we are never told whether the lawyer followed Jesus' admonition to "go and do likewise." If he did, was his life transformed by that and other acts of grace? If not, did he ever have another opportunity to be confronted by the possibilities of radical neighborliness and love? If he failed at this opportunity, did he become more rigid, legalistic, and dead in his faith? We do not know.

We can hope that he might have accepted Jesus' advice simply because he was sensitive enough to acknowledge the truth of Jesus' story. But, of course, the point of the story for you and me is not how the lawyer responded or how any of the fictional characters might have acted in a continued version of the story. The point is how we respond. The temptation for hearers of a story of this kind is to settle for an insight or to be intrigued with the artistry of the parable or with new knowledge about the circumstances surrounding it rather than plumbing it for new depths of faith and spiritual insight.

How might the lawyer have responded? In what way might this parable have transformed or entrenched his life?

Avoiding the Distractions of the "What Ifs"

I find that when I preach from this story, many people try to make an immediate application by recalling those instances when they have seen someone stalled on the highway with car trouble. This inevitably leads to a discussion of the hazards of helping someone on the highway: Is it a setup to rob the person who is good hearted enough to offer help? If the person is injured, would he or she sue you for improper medical assistance? The modern complications are many.

Let's not allow ourselves to be distracted by such questions, however. The point of this parable is not whether we should extend help to someone in trouble on the highway but that we should know how to fulfill the

Avoiding the Distractions of the "What Ifs" ■

Be careful not to let too many hypothetical questions interfere with the point of the story. What is the point of the story?

How do digressions disrupt the lessons of the faith?

great commandment—"Love your neighbor as yourself"—and should realize that Jesus Christ has extended our neighborhood to take in the whole human race.

The Parable and Me ■
What are some possible prior questions to "Who is my neighbor?"

What are your prior questions? How do you answer those questions?

The Parable and Me

How do I go about being a Christian neighbor? The Samaritan found his neighbor on the side of a road. Our neighbors are not usually thrust into our pathways in such dramatic fashion. Maybe we need to ask God to reveal our neighbors to us, for it is quite possible that we have grown so accustomed to passing by on the other side that we do not even see the opportunity for being a neighbor.

That is, many of us need to be made newly sensitive to the whole concept of the Christian neighbor. Often we are thoughtful and attentive to those in our circle of friendship without ever realizing how little we do for others outside that special group.

Perhaps there is a prior question. Many of us today are so busy with home, work, school, children, church, clubs, sports, and a host of other activities that we not only do not know our neighbors, we do not want to know them. Is the idea of neighborliness even on our minds? Are we so concerned or consumed with the needs and demands of living our own lives, even of surviving day by day, that we feel we do not have time, energy, or intention to see anyone except our loved ones as our own concern?

We may also see this parable from the perspective of the victim rather than from the perspective of one who is scrambling to understand if the Samaritan helped appropriately or if the priest and Levite could justify having turned away. Repeated victimization and marginalization does not create an attitude of neighborliness in the one so treated.

Look at the story from what might be the victim's point of view.

What issues might affect the victim in deciding if he or she is willing to be considered a neighbor? What issues do victimization or marginalization raise in terms of our ability to be willing to accept or be a neighbor?

Review the questions in the main text. How would you answer them?

How might this parable encourage you to make or renew your commitment to Jesus Christ? If you wish, pray a renewing prayer to God.

Close With Prayer ■

Ask who knows someone (nearby or faraway) who needs a neighbor. After such needs have been listed, try to include each need in the closing prayer. If there are numerous requests, this prayer could be offered in smaller groups. Conclude each prayer with a commitment to be God's neighbor to someone, somewhere during the course of the coming week.

The Samaritan was willing to close the distance between himself and the injured traveler. Was the traveler equipped to have that distance closed? What fears were implanted and what prejudices were reinforced by the attack? Could one act of kindness wipe away layers of entrenched distrust? Was the victim thus empowered to close the distance of animosity and rejection between him and future thieves of his personal dignity and civil rights?

A good exercise this week would be to ask God in our daily prayers to help us see where our "neighbor" might be, to ask for the sensitivity to understand whatever wounds our neighbor has received at our hands, and to pray for healing of our own injuries and for renewed trust in our neighbors.

Session Six

The Widow and the Unjust Judge
Luke 18:1-8

Session Focus ■

All of us seem to believe in prayer, but most of us readily confess that we do not pray as much as we ought to pray. This chapter is intended to encourage consistent, undiscouraged prayer. Its truths can be applied to both personal and public concerns, for in both instances we are often inclined to give up too soon.

Session Objective ■

This session should help us appreciate more deeply the importance of prayer in all of life; and it should result not only in thinking about prayer, but in improvements in our prayer life.

Session Preparation ■

A study on prayer requires not only an intellectual grasp of the materials, but a deep-down feeling as well. That is, this subject calls for preparation of spirit as well as of mind. Try to read at least one short but inspiring book on prayer this week.

Some parables challenge us to search for the message. Today, however, we are studying a parable that declares its theme at the very outset. As we read the story, we may be tempted to get sidetracked by incidental issues; but the Gospel writer makes clear from the beginning why Jesus spoke the parable and why we ought to pay attention to it: "Then Jesus told them a parable about their need to pray always and not to lose heart" (Luke 18:1). We know where this story is going.

A Battle of Wills

It is a fascinating little story and one that must have gotten immediate response from Jesus' audience. When Jesus described this certain judge "who neither feared God nor had respect for people," most of Jesus' listeners probably had someone in mind.

The person in the parable was not a Jewish judge; ordinary Jewish litigation was taken to the elders for a decision. Some of the paid Roman magistrates were infamous for their indifference to justice and their readiness to accept and even to solicit bribes.

A popular saying was that many of these Roman judges would pervert justice for a dish of meat. People relished making a pun on their title in the Greek, where by dropping a

Session Outline ■

Before opening this session with prayer, note that the topic under discussion is prayer and that we should therefore approach it with a particularly prayerful attitude. Receive prayer requests, and be sure to include them in the opening prayer.

A Battle of Wills ■

Do you know someone who "neither fears God nor respects people"? How do you feel about him or her?

What life circumstances did widows face in Jesus' day? What kind of support and power did they have in their society? How is their situation similar to or different from widows (and widowers) today?

What seemed to be her greatest asset, according to the story?

Read Luke 18:1-8 and use a commentary on Luke to gain a deeper understanding. Recap the story. What happened?

What was the judge's response to the woman's persistence? Have you ever had a response such as this paraphrase in the text? If so, what happened?

single letter they could change the word from "judges of punishment" to "robber judges."

And to just such a judge, a widow came. She could hardly have been a more helpless candidate. With no man to care for her, a first-century widow was thrown on the mercy of charity at best or of crime at worst.

This widow was a dramatic symbol of all who were poor and unable to protect their meager rights. Widows then did not have insurance, nor were they guaranteed an inheritance from their husband's estate. Women bereft of spouse relied on the largesse of their sons or the brothers or near kinsmen of their departed husband. This widow may have had all or none of what little "safety net" her culture provided.

But the widow did have at least one thing going for her: her own indomitable spirit out of which emerged a fierce persistence. She had no one else, it seemed, to plead her cause; so she threw herself into the battle with everything that was in her.

I would like to describe this woman as a fighting tiger; but in truth, she was more like a pesky terrier. She could not really hurt the judge. His position came from Rome, and Roman authorities were not overly concerned about complaints from little Jewish widows. But perhaps her very feistiness unnerved the judge. It seems he met his match, and she "out-stubborned" him.

William Barclay tells us that when the judge says that he fears she will wear him out by her continual coming, he is using a Greek word that was often translated "give me a black eye." Perhaps the judge was overweight and out of condition, living a self-indulgent life; and this perky, persistent woman had a fire in her eye that worried him.

So the judge opted for expediency. I can

hear him explaining it to some of his friends at a professional gathering: "All of you know that I am not afraid of anyone, either God or men. But I tell you, she's getting to me. Everywhere I turn, she seems to be there. I know she can't do me any harm. Not really. But at this rate, she could give me an ulcer.

"So I'm going to vindicate her. The fact is, she has a good case. I'm giving her what she's asking for."

At this point in the story some people in the crowd perhaps broke into spontaneous applause, while others chuckled or smiled appreciatively. They liked the way this story turned out.

Pay Attention to the Verdict

This is the kind of story that called for immediate interpretation, otherwise the people would be content just to enjoy its human elements (perhaps by applying it to Roman judges they knew). So though Jesus often concluded parables without any word of interpretation, this time he hurried to his point: "Listen to what the unrighteous judge says. And will not God grant justice to his chosen ones who cry to him day and night?" (Luke 18:6-7).

Many who read this story are so troubled by one question that they miss the point of the story itself. Why, they ask, is God compared with an unjust judge, a brutal and merciless man? And the answer, of course, is that God is not compared with this judge. God is portrayed in contrast to the judge. If even an unjust judge will show mercy when he is persistently pursued, how much more will God vindicate "his chosen ones"?

Jesus' initial statements about his mission and ministry indicate his priority to the Jews. Later he and the disciples branch out; and, of course, after the Resurrection, Jesus sent his

Pay Attention to ■
the Verdict

The story calls for immediate interpretation, but what can happen if we leap to a quick judgment?

Who do the characters in the parable represent? What does this parable suggest about its characters?

How does God compare and contrast to the judge in this story?

Who are the elect in the story? What does that mean for us today? Has your cultural group been affected by being considered among the "elect"? by being considered outside the "elect"? What has been the result? What can you do about it?

disciples to all nations. But at this point, the Jews understood themselves to be the chosen nation, the elect. God selected them for the Promised Land and pledged to them offspring and ongoing relationship. Inherently understood in that covenant was that God's people would live and work faithfully and seek God through worship and prayer. That they often fell short of the conditions of their election was troublesome.

The point of the story is also troublesome, especially with regard to certain theories of prayer. The stated issue of the story, clear and inescapable, is that we should not give up in our praying; we ought "to pray always and not . . . lose heart."

Persistent Prayer

Why should we pray so persistently? Is it necessary to convince God of our earnestness? Or is God indifferent to our prayers? Must we convince God of the rightness of our cause and of our need of divine help?

If this were the only place in the Scriptures where we are taught to "pray without ceasing," we might perhaps find a way around the issue (though doing so would surely take some artful maneuvering). But this theme of unwavering prayer comes up again and again in both the Old and the New Testaments.

Why? Part of the answer is suggested in the concluding sentence of the parable, as Jesus asks if the Son of Man will find faith when he comes. Our prayers help to sustain our faith. In a world where the powers of evil assert themselves so constantly and destructively, we need support from outside ourselves. Prayer solicits such power. But more than that, by the very act of prayer we engage ourselves in the faith experience. We cannot hope to have enough faith to see us through the long peri-

Persistent Prayer ■
How would you respond to these questions?

What does the whole body of Scriptures teach us about prayer?

What kind of power is there in prayer?

What is the purpose of prayer? What, in your experience, is the result of prayer?

Is your discipline of prayer what you would like it to be?

What are the barriers to prayer? to persistence in prayer?

Read Isaiah 40:31. What does it suggest to you about prayer?

Engaging Prayer Against Evil

How does prayer engage evil?

List on a chalkboard or paper matters that people prayed for over a period of generations that have now been solved, such as a cure for polio, and those for which we have prayed but for which the answer has not yet come, such as world peace. How large a part did prayer play in solving those problems that have been worked out ? How should we pray regarding matters like world peace and an end to hunger?

Do you see prayer as a kind of partnership with God? Do you feel as if you are in some way a partner with God? Explain.

ods of waiting unless we follow a continuing practice of prayer. It is by communing with God, and thus making ourselves sensitive to the eternal, that we get the strength to manage all those things that are only temporary. It is hard to say, "This, too, will pass" unless we are encouraged through our relationship to God to hope for a better, eternal day.

Thus, when we pray, we are restoring our own spirits. The great Hebrew prophet promised that those who "wait upon the Lord" find themselves renewed; and the renewing equips us to rise up like eagles, run, or walk, whatever the demands of life may be (Isaiah 40:31).

Engaging Prayer Against Evil

But prayer does more than change the mind and manner of the person who prays. When we pray, we engage in the eternal struggle against evil. Far from arguing with God to convince him of the rightness of our wishes, prayer, at its best, puts us in alliance with God for the achieving of his purposes.

We accept this principle in our actions and words, but we are somehow reluctant to apply the same principle to our prayers. When we raise food or money for hunger programs or lobby for legislation that will provide opportunities for the poor, we are consciously engaged in the battle against evil. So, too, when we struggle against the easy availability of obscene and pornographic materials. And also, of course, when we labor for world peace. We recognize that war, hunger, ignorance, and brutality are manifestations of evil; and we throw ourselves into action against them.

We are consistent when we involve ourselves in these same struggles through the avenue of prayer. By our praying we declare

When we say, in the Lord's Prayer, "Your will be done," is this a sign of resignation or is it a cry for victory? Explain.

Does God answer prayer? Does God answer your prayers? If so, how? If you think God is unresponsive, why do you think so?

ourselves to be partners with God in pursuing God's will. Indeed, isn't that the very theme of that portion of the Lord's Prayer that appeals,

> Your kingdom come,
> Your will be done,
>   on earth as it is in heaven. (Matthew 6:10)?

Each time we speak that phrase, we acknowledge that the will of God is not currently being carried out in our world. And we also declare that we think our prayers can play a part in bringing God's will to pass. We believe that God hears us.

If we concede that this is the case, we can understand more clearly why the parable urges us, by the example of the insistent widow, to keep on crying for relief. This is no time to give up in the struggle against evil and in our pursuit of the will of God. We must continue both to work and to pray until the battle is won.

Vindication ∎

What does "vindication" or "granting justice" mean to you? What does it mean in this parable?

Vindication

One of the most interesting terms in this parable is "grant her justice," which some other versions of the Bible translate as "vindicate." This idea appears three times, in quick succession: The judge says that he will grant justice to (vindicate) the woman; then Jesus assures us that God will "grant justice to his chosen ones"; and more than that, Jesus assures us that God will "quickly grant justice to them."

In what ways might we benefit as a society and in the world if we had a more biblical image of granting justice?

This is a term and an insight that appears often in the Book of Psalms. Some of the psalms that we find most difficult to understand because they seem bent on unworthy vengeance are built around this cry for vindication. The idea of the Hebrew word was "render me the justice due to me." Even in the best of systems it is often difficult for the poor and the disadvantaged to obtain justice, and this was especially so in much of the Middle Eastern world in ancient times.

Thus the people in Jesus' audience understood fully what the Master was saying when he promised that the widow would receive vindication. It was a goal most of them had sought and had found difficult to achieve. Now the Great Teacher was saying that God was hearing their prayers and that justice would indeed come their way.

But many of us have difficulty seeking vindication—the justice we deserve—without being caught up in vindictiveness. Rightly the Scriptures remind us that vengeance is God's business, not ours. We do not understand the right and wrong of most issues clearly enough to mete out vengeance we think ought to be poured out on others, and it is quite possible that someone else is imagining what judgment we should receive.

Vengeance and vindication are often too volatile and hazardous to be trusted to our human fallibility. Nevertheless, we need to be reassured that God is conscious of the issue and that heaven is at work to set right that which is wrong.

What is the difference between vindication and vindictiveness?

What is vengeance?

What is God's role in justice? in vindictiveness? in vengeance?

The Reality of Evil

Do you believe in a distinct force of evil in the world? If so, how would you describe it? What evidence do you see for or against a force of evil?

Is the judge in the story a force for good or for evil (or for neither)? What makes you think so?

It seems to me that this parable may be concerned, not simply with the particular individuals or governments that are unjust, but with the primary fact that we live in a world where evil is at work in many forms. Ultimately, the enemy is not a particular political party or individual, and not even necessarily a particular political or economic philosophy, but the root fact of evil. This evil expresses itself through individuals and institutions. But evil is more pervasive than that, especially when we consider those attitudes that make life difficult—fear, prejudice, apathy, resentment, despair.

So we live in a world where evil manifests itself in many ways. We are like the widow who was beset by an adversary greater than she was and who looked to the magistrate for relief. The ultimate relief, Jesus taught, will be in the coming kingdom of heaven. But meanwhile we labor and pray for spreading outposts of that Kingdom, and we pray for that Kingdom to come. And Jesus urged, Don't give up! Vindication will come.

This parable is a powerful reassurance in a world where evil seems sometimes to run rampant. It must have been particularly bracing to the generation that first received copies of Luke's Gospel, for by that time the tiny band of believers was again and again being victimized by persecution. In the midst of attacks by powerful governments that were not overly concerned with justice or fair play, believers were promised that God cared and was at work to set things right.

Where is God, do you think, in the midst of sin and when life seems out of control?

This is also a reassuring word at certain times in our personal life when we feel that circumstances have gotten out of control. William Cowper was one of the most talented poets of the eighteenth century and was also a devout Christian. But he suffered from periods of dark depression in which he was driven to the edge of despair. It was probably as a result of such a time that Cowper wrote the poem that includes these lines:

> But trust Him for his grace;
> Behind a frowning providence
> He hides a smiling face.
> ("Olney Hymns, LXVIII")

Perhaps at times Cowper saw God as the unjust judge. But faith had taught him to remember that God was faithfully at work, even behind that seeming frown.

How Long, O Lord?

However, there is the factor of time and the difference between God's view of time and ours. Jesus promised, "I tell you he will

How Long, O Lord? ■

What does "quickly" mean in this parable? What does it mean to you?

How do you understand God's time? How does that affect your faith? your understanding of prayer? your willingness to pray?

vindicate them speedily." It is clear enough that "speedily" has a differfent definition for those who are waiting. "How long, O Lord," the weary Old Testament saint cried, "How long?" What is God's measure of time, and how are we to respond to it?

We are often reminded that a day with the Lord is as a thousand years to us and a thousand years as a day. That is noble to say, but it does not help very much when the rent is due tomorrow. In most of the business of our life, we would be glad if God would start working according to our calendars. And I do not think it is wrong to ask God to be concerned with our timeline. After all, Jesus assured us that God notes the fall of a sparrow and that the very hairs of our heads are numbered. The Lord is not indifferent to the everyday humanness of our life. God knows that most of the time our problems have to do, not with issues of the centuries, but with matters here and now.

But often, of course, you and I are like little children in our concept of time. We think we cannot possibly wait until tomorrow, when in truth tomorrow may be a far better time for the answer than today. We are often inclined to break the cocoons of life before the butterfly is ready to come forth. We pray, "Act speedily"; but in many instances God's best answer may well be, "Tomorrow will be a better time."

How speediy do you do what you understand to be God's will?

Do you think that in time of prayer God addresses petitions or intercessions to you (as well as you asking God to intercede)? If so, might God hope to have those petitions fulfilled quickly by you?

And sometimes, of course, we are ourselves the greatest impediment to the answering of our prayers. We plead, "Hurry, Lord," while we are ourselves dragging our feet. That is why our prayers should include time for listening to God and for soul searching. In such times of holy introspection we may discover how to be the instrument for answering our prayers and how to wait productively.

How might God feel if we drag our feet to respond? What does this mean to you?

When we pray for great social and economic causes, such as peace, justice, and relief from

What, if anything, is the relationship between prayer and science? prayer and teaching? Prayer and social justice? Is there any sphere of influence in which prayer cannot play a viable part? Explain.

What other "unjust judges" can you name besides disease and ignorance? What or who are the "widows" who challenge them persistently?

Will Christ Find Faith?

What is the point of the parable for Jesus' hearers? What is the point for you? What, if anything, will it motivate you to do, think, or believe?

What does it mean to you to "not lose heart"?

In what ways does your faith energize you?

When, if ever, have you been tempted to give up in something really too important to give up on? What happened? Did prayer play a part?

The Parable and Me

Do you find that you are tempted to give up praying too soon and to give up too soon teaching, serving, and loving? If so, what lesson does the widow have to teach?

poverty, we need to have the long view. The late Ernest Fremong Tittle said that those who pray should learn from the scientist. Medical research, he said, "is a prayer for the relief of suffering and the abolition of disease"; and the scientist perseveres in that prayer no matter what the odds or what the delay. I look upon teachers the same way. In the classroom they make their "prayer" against ignorance. It is sometimes a discouraging task, but like the widow of Jesus' parable, they have to hold on until they win. Ignorance and disease, after all, are unjust judges; they fear neither God nor men. But such foes can be worn down by earnest persistence.

Will Christ Find Faith?

But when the Son of man comes, Jesus said, "will he find faith on earth?" In a sense the point of this parable is not the answer to prayer, but the unceasing faithfulness of the widow. As it happens, she got her answer; and Jesus assured his disciples that they, too, will receive the answer just because God is better by far than the unjust judge. But Jesus did not conclude the parable by asking, "Will your prayers be unanswered?" or by promising an answer. The final word is a question addressed to our commitment: When Jesus comes, will he find us faithful?

Perhaps the secular person can be forgiven, or at least understood, for losing heart in life's struggle. But those of us who believe are energized to keep on working and praying. Believers are thus the hope of the world, under God. We are sure that God is with us in our quest for the kingdom of heaven; so we can rightly pray, in the language of Harry Emerson Fosdick,

Save us from weak resignation
To the evils we deplore...

What happens when "the good people get tired of being good before the bad people get tired of being bad"? Does prayer matter here?

Consider taking a time of prayer now to make or affirm your commitment to Jesus Christ.

Close With Prayer ■

Invite each person to share some longstanding prayer need, so that everyone can embrace it with faith and caring. These needs can be either personal or community and worldwide. If you wish, list the needs so that group members can remember them in their prayers through the coming week.

Pray together this prayer from *The Imitation of Christ,* by Thomas á Kempis:

"Grant me, O Lord, to know that which is worth knowing, to love that which is worth loving, to praise that which pleaseth Thee most, to esteem that which to Thee seemeth precious, to abhor that which in Thy sight is unclean. Suffer me not to judge according to the sight of the outward eyes, nor to give sentence according to the hearing of the ears of ignorant men; but with a true judgment to discern between things visible and spiritual, and above all to be ever searching after the good pleasure of Thy will."

as we seek the wisdom and courage "for the facing of this hour." Like the persistent widow, we will not give up.

The Parable and Me

I feel that we can apply this parable at two levels of life, prayer and service. And as we do, perhaps we should remind ourselves that the two are closely related. For both are necessary to bring the kingdom of God to pass.

And we are tempted to give up on both. We stop praying too soon and we stop teaching, serving, and loving too soon.

Jesus commended the widow because she persevered even though everything in life seemed stacked against her. Her cause was right, but this is not why she won; as a matter of fact, many "right" causes are lost even though they deserve to win. She won because she simply refused to give up. That is the spirit Jesus encourages in us, as we throw ourselves into the battle against evil.

I think often of the instance at the turn of the century when a coalition of dedicated citizens tried to overturn a corrupt political machine in New York City. At first, they won; then after a short period of time the political machine was back in power. Someone wisely explained that this happened because "the good people got tired of being good before the bad people got tired of being bad."

So we need to learn from the persevering widow. Her goodness outlasted the evil judge's badness. And we need to remember Jesus' appeal that we should alway pray and not lose heart. For our praying not only brings victory in the struggle against evil, it also saves us from losing heart.

The Wise and Foolish Bridesmaids Matthew 25:1-13

Many of the people of Jesus' day saw religion as a generally burdensome thing. The Ten Commandments were manageable, but the hundreds of additions and refinements of the law that religious leaders had added to the commandments made life difficult.

In a sense, we are not too different from those first-century Jews. The key watchwords of the Christian faith are such terms as *love, joy, peace, hope*, and *faith*; but we often act as if the prevailing theme were demands, requirements, and restrictions.

Come to the Wedding

To such a world Jesus one day said, "The kingdom of heaven is like a wedding party!" That was not only good news to his audience, it was nearly unbelievable news. In the first-century Middle East, weddings were the major social and celebrative event. A wedding was more than a matter of food, fun, laughter, dancing, and gift giving; the event was so significant that the bride and groom were excused from even major religious duties. A rabbi could forsake his study of the law in order to attend a wedding feast. According to a popular Jewish saying, "Everyone from six to sixty will follow the marriage drum."

Session Outline ■

Receive prayer requests and causes for thanksgiving from the group; then lead in an opening prayer that seeks wisdom from God and an openness of spirit.

Come to the ■ Wedding

What do you know about weddings in this biblical era? Use a Bible dictionary for extra information. How are these celebrations similar to and different from your experience?

Read Matthew 25:1-13. What do you learn about wedding practices and the inclusion of guests at the celebration?

Roleplay the story if you wish. We can imagine the opening visit to the oil merchant, who urged the foolish girls to buy more oil, and their somewhat flippant refusal. Then, the casual conversation with the five wise companions, until the bridegroom's announcement is heard. We follow them through their pleading with their fellow watchers, their trip back to the merchant ("I told you so!"), and at last to the refusal of entrance.

But the prospect of joy is also always the prospect of disappointment. Even the best of news has a kind of threat in it, for there is the chance that perhaps you will miss the event or that it will be less than you expected.

So Jesus told a story from the vantage point, not of the bride and groom, but of ten young women who had been invited to the happy occasion. Five of them, Jesus said, were foolish; and five were wise. What was the measure of their wisdom? In a word, their readiness to be part of the event. And their readiness was measured in their supply of oil. All the young women had oil in their lamps, but the wise ones had an additional supply in their oil flasks.

This element of preparedness in the story is foreign to our idea of a wedding party. Weddings in our society are announced for a specific time and place; and if the ceremony is more than five or six minutes late in starting, the assembled group begins to fidget. But in first-century Palestine, a wedding could happen anytime within several days or even a fortnight. The uncertainty was part of the excitement. The bridegroom hoped to catch some of the bridal party napping.

And Be Ready

But fairness required that there be an announcement. A man was to go through the streets shouting, "Behold, the bridegroom is coming." The alert ones would be ready enough to respond. The others would be left behind.

In Jesus' parable, the cry came at midnight. Such was often the case, for bridegrooms frequently chose a nighttime appearance. The sleeping attendants were awakened by the warning cry and began quickly to trim their lamps. At that moment, the

What happens at this point in the parable?

What was the response of the young women who had enough oil?

Can you recall some instance where you had to run to an all night market in order to take care of some errand that had been overlooked during the normal hours of the day? Did you find what you needed? Have you ever had to get to a store (such as a pharmacy) that wasn't open when you really needed it to be?

What does this passage tell you about the importance of readiness for life's emergencies? for the daily routines of life?

Sufficient Oil ■

Who is this parable for?

What is the significance of the bridesmaids being virgins in this story? How might we describe them today?

foolish girls realized that they did not have enough oil to get them through the night. "Give us some of your oil," they begged their friends, "for our lamps are going out."

The prepared ones answered in a way that at first seems selfish or at least hardhearted: "No! There will not be enough for you and for us; you had better go to the dealers and buy some for yourselves."

So the young women hurried out into the night. When they returned, the door was shut. They appealed desperately for admission. But the bridegroom was cold in his refusal. "I don't know you," he said. That is, "If you belonged at this event, you would already be here."

Jesus' conclusion to the story is also its message: "Keep awake therefore, for you know neither the day nor the hour" (Matthew 25:13). The issue of the story, as we suggested earlier, is *readiness*. When God announces the grand celebration, will I be ready? In the manner of the oriental bridegroom, God may "come" or appear at any time. I need an adequate supply of oil.

Sufficient Oil

This is a parable for believers. It is not intended to make a distinction between believers and nonbelievers; it is intended to warn believers that they must constantly be attentive to the state of their soul if they are to fulfill the purposes of God. All ten of the young bridesmaids, both foolish and wise, were virgins, according to numerous Bible translations; and, of course, virginity is a biblical symbol of purity. All ten had an invitation to the wedding, and they were all waiting expectantly for the bridegroom. And all ten had a measure of oil (oil is a standard biblical symbol for the Holy Spirit).

What is the significance of the oil and of having enough for the lamps? How might we describe that today?

What is the difference, in the parable, between the two groups of young women?

What does it mean to "not make it on somebody else's oil"? In what ways have you ever tried to "borrow someone else's oil"? What was the result over the short term? over the long term? What has happened when someone else has tried "to make it on your oil"?

The only difference between the girls was the measure of preparedness. All these young women had oil in their lamps, but the wise ones had an extra supply that would see them through the long night.

As indicated earlier, when we first read this parable, we are troubled by the unwillingness of the wise bridesmaids to share their extra supply of oil. We need to look behind their answer to a hard fact of life: You and I cannot make it on somebody else's oil. We can help one another in so many ways, but at some point every soul is on its own. Ultimately, we cannot get by on our parents' religion or on that of our pastor, Sunday school teacher, or dear friend. We have to go to God's market and buy for ourselves. There is no such thing as secondhand Christianity.

So the foolish women went to the market. I see them awakening the seller of oil, despite the midnight hour. But when they returned, the door was closed. The celebration had begun, and they were outside.

In my boyhood I heard more than one evangelistic sermon that warned that we too might be late in making a decision to follow Christ. Some of those appeals were overly dramatic, and probably some people could reason after a few years that the argument was false. After all, they had heard it so many times; and they were still around to hear it again.

And in truth, life generally grants us many opportunities. We can ignore one knock at the heart's door or one grand invitation and be almost sure that someday, somewhere, there will be another. In most of the issues of life, opportunity comes to us again and again. And surely God, in lovingkindness, makes repeated and insistent calls.

Is it ever too late to try to come to God's kingdom? Explain?

The Wise and Foolish Bridesmaids **81**

An old adage says that three things, once gone, do not return; and one of those is the opportunity left unimproved. Do you believe this? What has your experience taught you? What does the parable say?

The Bridegroom Is Coming ■

What is the wedding banquet describing in this parable?

What does the Bible tell us about the return of the Christ? What do you believe about it? about the Kingdom?

But it is also true that a time comes that is the last time. All life's opportunities have a possibility of finality about them, insofar as we understand life. And in that respect the preachers were right when they warned that our response might sometime be "too late." The parable under study warns us of that harsh but real fact.

The Bridegroom Is Coming

The major point of this parable, of course, is the importance of being ready for our Lord's coming. The feast or wedding banquet was a familiar image of the heavenly realm where all whom God brought to the table in faith would feast in glory. In Jesus' day it was considered quite an affront to the host either to turn down the invitation or to fail, for whatever reason, to attend. The grand fete is not just for the host; it is in the guest's best interest to attend and to receive the gift of hospitality.

This great wedding feast no doubt is meant to describe the occasion when God's plan is made complete in the ultimate triumph of our Lord. This time of fulfillment and glorification of believers was eagerly sought after. But we sometimes have a hard time dealing with this subject because it has been abused and even exploited by those who have tried to set dates for our Lord's return. The long wait may also make us blasé about its actual coming; Jesus' hearers and first-generation Christians felt its immediacy more than most of us.

The most flagrant abusers have actually identified a specific day or year, but more have settled for saying that "all the signs are fulfilled" and that this generation or even this decade will be the time of Jesus' coming. I have lived long enough to remember those

Have you ever been encouraged to believe that the Second Coming was imminent? Do you think it is? How might you interpret the fact that it has not yet come to pass?

who taught that Mussolini was the antichrist and his nation the fulfillment of prophecies in Daniel and Revelation, so I am especially sensitive to the issue.

Since then, there have been numerous other wars over religion, crude oil, ethnicity, territory; the rich continue to exploit the poor; disrespect for others and their property is rampant; we seem time and again to be plowing fertile ground for the seeds of evil. As we approach and attain the new millennium, no doubt there will be other predictions of the ultimate fullness of time (And they could be true!); only God knows for sure.

But in this matter, as in so many others, we must be careful not to throw out the baby with the bath water. However much certain types of preaching or teaching may address, even mishandle, the subject of Christ's return, we must remember that the return is a legitimate part of Jesus' teaching. The fact that some may—intentionally or unintentionally—abuse the subject should not cause us to neglect it. Our Lord's warning is as valid as ever: "Keep awake therefore, for you know neither the day nor the hour." And it is precisely because we do not know (and neither do the most enthusiastic or sincere Bible teachers) that we ought to be constantly attentive.

Seize Opportunities

Seize Opportunities

Have you ever tried to make up for a lack of preparedness by some "last-minute shopping"?

In a sense, too, this parable can be applied to many other crises of life. One of the most obvious is the time prior to major surgery. Such an occasion may reveal a dramatic shortage in our supply of oil. As a parish pastor, I have known many instances where people wanted to make up for years of neglect by some frantic last-minute shopping. At

What opportunities have you had and do you have to "shop for oil"? What have you done or do you plan to do with those opportunities?

such times I do my best to help. But I sometimes feel as the oil merchant must have in Jesus' parable: I wish they had done their shopping earlier!

I remember a family long ago, in an early parish of mine, who wanted me to counsel their daughter who was about to make a decision they felt was wrong. We visited for half an hour, and I did my best to point out some of the issues involved in the young woman's decision; but she chose still to go contrary to what her parents (rightly, I think) saw as the best course. Afterward the mother suggested, somewhat reproachfully, that she had hoped I would be able to turn her daughter in the right direction. I wanted to answer (but didn't), "I'm not able to do in thirty minutes what you neglected to do for thirty years."

In a sense, a major purpose of every worship service, every prayer group, and every Sunday school class is to give us a chance to shop for oil. These occasions provide opportunity for us to equip ourselves for the Lord's coming. For our Lord returns, not only in the grand consummation of human history, but in the continuing challenges and opportunities of daily life. And in each instance, we need the oil of the Holy Spirit to lighten our way.

Supposedly when Mary of Orange was dying, her court chaplain tried to show her the way of salvation. Mary answered, "I have not left this matter to this hour." In that reply, she was speaking the language of the wise virgins of Jesus' parable. Matters of eternity are too important to be left to the last minute. One wonders why we do so.

If you are ready to affirm or to reaffirm your commitment to Christ, pray silently for God to seal that covenant.

The Response of Folly

What is "folly" or "foolishness" in biblical terms? How would you describe "wisdom"? What is the difference that makes the five bridesmaids foolish and the other five wise? Is foolishness a sin? Explain.

The Response of Folly

Jesus' explanation, in a word, is that we are "foolish." I have to remind myself that the five women who missed the grand event were neither bad nor immoral; they were just "foolish."

Wisdom and foolishness, in biblical usage, both have a moral content. It is not a matter of scholastic knowledge; it is an issue of right values and of productive living. And above all else, it is the question of our relationship to God and eternity. A scholar who lives as if there is no God would be a fool in the biblical view. After all, it is "fools" who say in their heart, "There is no God," as the psalmist reports it (Psalm 53:1).

And wisdom means living with the long view. The measure of light is not the convenience of the moment. Wisdom looks for consequences and values down the road a way and especially for the measure of eternity. Good and pure as they were, the foolish virgins were shortsighted. They wanted to attend the wedding supper, but they had not thought through the price.

What has been the consequence of your own occasions of foolishness? What price might you have to pay for lack of preparedness in a crucial decision or issue?

Their error reminds us of Jesus' lesson of the builder and the warrior. No one, he said, should go into battle unless he has calculated whether he can win; and no one should begin building a tower unless he realizes how much it will take to complete the job. Jesus doesn't call such persons "fools," but that is the word that immediately comes to a person's mind: "What a foolish thing to do, to begin something you aren't prepared to finish!"

The Rich Fool

The Rich Fool

Read the parable of the rich fool in Luke 12:16-21. Use a commentary to gain deeper understanding. What is the gist of the story?

In another parable Jesus uses such language and uses it vigorously. As a matter of fact, we usually refer to it as the parable of the rich fool. The story (Luke 12:16-21) tells of a well-to-do farmer whose operation was proceeding so beautifully that he hardly

What does this parable have to do with the parable of the ten bridesmaids?

knew how to handle all his success. With a series of bumper crops, he had run out of storage space. He came out with what appeared to be a sensible, farseeing conclusion: "I will pull down my barns and build larger ones." But Jesus said that in the eyes of God, the man was a fool. That very night his soul was "demanded" of him.

On the surface, this story seems to have little to do with the story of the wise and foolish bridesmaids. After all, as we have already noted, these foolish women were not bad people; their very description as "virgins" is the biblical way to prove their character. The rich man, on the other hand, does not seem especially admirable.

But the two stories have two significant elements in common. For one, they both end in the ultimate tragedy of souls that were not ready to meet their Lord and were therefore shut out of the beauty God had intended for them. And, of course, the other factor in common is that in both parables persons are described as conducting their lives foolishly.

How would you describe the vision of the rich man? Does he seem foolish to you? Explain.

Perhaps the two parables are indicating that we may miss the purpose and plan of God for quite different reasons. The rich man was, from a human, business point of view, farseeing in his planning. He was able to see beyond the current market and the present market prices. But he could not see beyond this world, this harvest, or the prospects of the stock and commodity market.

Prepare for Tomorrow and for Today

Does *tomorrow* seems like a dangerous word to you? Why or why not?

Prepare for Tomorrow and for Today

The five young women probably come to mind as a giddy, happy-go-lucky quintet, so absorbed in the excitement of the coming wedding that they simply have not thought through the practical matter of their oil supply. You would be more likely to trust your investments with the rich farmer than with the young women. But you would not dare trust your soul to them. They all, in their own ways, had the short view.

William Barclay, the Bible teacher, once said that one of the most dangerous days in a person's life is when that person discovers the word *tomorrow*. In the sense in which Barclay meant it (as referring to procrastination), he was right. If we reason as the five girls did that we can always buy our oil tomorrow, we are in trouble.

But another attitude toward "tomorrow" is quite as bad from an eternal point of view. That is the attitude of the rich fool. He was overly conscious of tomorrow and was so absorbed in providing for his financial tomorrows that he made no provision for his soul today. He might well have told his pastor, "I'm the kind of person who looks ahead to be sure the future is taken care of." To which the counselor would have to reply, "But you are not looking far enough ahead."

"When the Son of Man comes," Jesus said in conclusion to another parable, "will he find faith on earth?" (Luke 18:8). Such is the question of this parable too. So many of the things that matter most in life call for a long wait. Faith is the virtue that enables us to endure the long periods of waiting. Our language once had a word, *staith*, that was meant to describe the quality of steadfastness, that facet of character that causes one to hold on for the long pull. It seems appropriate that it rhymes so well with "faith" because the two qualities are close kin. Those who have faith are more likely also to have staith. And they will be waiting when the Lord comes, whatever the nature of that coming may be—whether by death, a crisis of life, or the ultimate consummation of all things.

What does "tomorrow" mean from an eternal point of view? What does that suggest to you about the way you cultivate your prayer life or discipline yourself for Bible reading, for example?

How would you describe faith? the results or expression of faith?

In thinking about your own life, do you think that "when the Son of Man comes," he will find faith? In thinking about the church? about your community? your country? the earth?

The five foolish virgins are particularly appropriate to our times. Our culture is described as being committed to instant gratification. We want not only instant coffee and service but also instant fulfillment. Storing up oil for the long wait does not fit the current style. You and I will have to buck the spirit of the times if we are to live in such a way as to be ready when the bridegroom's call goes forth.

The Blessings of the Banquet

The Blessings of the Banquet ▪

What are the blessings of the banquet? Why would you want to be invited? Why would you want to attend?

But we must end this discussion of the negative. The warning is given to the foolishness in our nature so that we will work earnestly to avoid being shut out of life's best joys and eternity's possibilities. But we ought also to think about what is in store for those who are ready. Inside is the wedding feast: laughter, music, dancing, food. The prospect of blessing ought to stir us to dedicated living even more than the dangers of neglect.

And this is particularly so when the ultimate blessing is full communion with God. All of history, Jesus taught, is building toward a day when God's final purposes are accomplished. We want to be ready to be part of that grand day. We are headed to a wedding feast!

The Parable and Me

The Parable and Me ▪

What is the point of the parable for you?

The aim of this parable is to encourage us to be ready for our divine opportunities. The climaxing opportunity, of course, is the divine marriage supper; but life provides us with any number of lesser opportunities with each passing year.

How do we make ourselves ready? The parable uses the symbol of oil, which is a picture of the Holy Spirit. The Holy Spirit, like all of God's kind provision, is a gift. But the Spirit is a gift that we can prepare to receive.

How do you make yourself ready for God?

What are the daily habits that have proven effective for you in being prepared in your relationship to God? What habits would you like to cultivate or to strengthen?

No great mystery surrounds the receiving of this gift. We open ourselves to God by faithful attendance at worship and by daily habits that make God more real to us. When we set a time each day for reading the Bible and for prayer, it is as if we were going to the market to shop for oil.

Productive friendships are also very important. When I look back on the periods in my life when my faith grew most consistently, these were periods when I had a close circle of Christian friends with whom I shared regularly.

I have learned, too, the importance of sensitive self-examination. When I was still a teenager, I asked a godly man to write a message in my Bible. One of the key phrases he wrote was, "Keep confessed up." It is so important to clear away the debris of life's failings and shortcomings, and this is done best by confessing our sins and asking for a new start. I am not recommending morbid self-condemnation. Quite the contrary. The beauty of Christianity is that we are taught to look at ourselves clearly and honestly, then to deal with our shortcomings and to trust God for forgiveness.

Close With Prayer

Close with prayer for watchfulness and preparedness in both the great and the small opportunities. Consider using the words of one of your hymns on the theme of "preparedness" or "covenant."

The Pharisee and the Tax Collector
Luke 18:9-14

Session Focus ■

The sins of the spirit are more dangerous to most of us than the sins of the flesh. This is particularly true of those of us who want to be exemplary in our living. This session should compel us to examine our innermost thoughts and motives.

Session Objective ■

Our goal in this session is to become more perceptive about the nature of true religion, as Jesus himself would define it, and to become more sensitive to the dangers of misusing religious faith.

Session Preparation ■

Look up *Pharisee* and *tax collector* in a Bible dictionary. Bring the definitions to the session as an aid to discussion. Also, look up *sinner* in a dictionary and in a book of quotations; see if these references provide some insights into the nature of the sins of the mind and spirit.

As we study the teachings of Jesus, we sometimes get the feeling that Jesus did not like so-called religious people. In the parable of the good Samaritan, for example, the two villains are professional religious workers. And in the story of the father and his two sons, the unsympathetic figure is the older brother who remained at home and was morally good but who exhibited a bitter and unloving attitude. Jesus' most severe words of condemnation were not directed against tax collectors and sinners but against some of the scribes and Pharisees, who were presumably the best-behaved people in town and those who should have understood God's will most clearly.

Righteous to a Fault

A smug, self-congratulatory, self-satisfied display of religion appears in this parable of the Pharisee and the tax collector. The central theme of the story is made clear at the very outset: "He also told this parable to some who trusted in themselves that they were righteous and regarded others with contempt" (Luke 18:9). The target of the story is evident.

This kind of story must have fascinated Jesus' audience. Two men, he said, were

Righteous to a Fault ■

Review briefly the character of the Pharisee. What is his history? What was the typical Pharisee like in his day?

What image have you held about the Pharisees and what they must have been like?

going to the Temple to pray. This was a common sight, for in those days the devout prayed at 9 A.M., noontime, and 3 P.M. Prayers at the Temple were thought to be more effective than those prayed elsewhere, so people who were able went to that sacred setting for their prayers. Of the two men, the one was a Pharisee, the other a tax collector.

First-century audiences were quite familiar with the images presented by these two kinds of people. Some Pharisees were sternly self-righteous, but no one could seriously question their earnestness. In truth, the Pharisees as a whole were the best defenders of their nation's religious heritage; in a sense, they were Israel's finest patriots. In fact, the Pharisees' origins hail back to the traumatic time in Israel's history when the Jews were under fierce persecution—what we would call the intertestamental period.

The Jews faced a brutal time, particularly under the reign of the Selucid ruler Antiochus IV Epiphanes. The intertestamental books of the Maccabees tell the story of the rise of Judas Maccabeus and his followers who were willing to be martyred rather than capitulate to Greek idolatry and other desecrations of the faith. The Hasadim were those loyal and faithful Jews who actively fought against the oppression; they were the forerunners of the Pharisees of Jesus' day.

The Pharisees were honest and upright, no doubt about it. If a Pharisee was your next-door neighbor, you would not have to worry about the safety of your belongings. Put in modern terms, you could have bought a used car from a Pharisee.

Why, as the Gospels describe them, do the Pharisees seem unpopular?

Nevertheless, the Pharisees were not very popular. Respected, yes, but popular, no. Some Pharisees were pretentious at times, and they often paraded their goodness.

Undoubtedly many ordinary people were made uncomfortable by the fact that the Pharisees were so scrupulous in their conduct. People who were not Pharisees probably had the uneasy feeling that they were always considered just slightly inferior.

An Unpopular Occupation ▪

Now review the character of the typical tax collector in Jesus' day. What was he like? Why did the Jews hate him so?

An Unpopular Occupation

But if the common people in Jesus' crowd found the Pharisees sometimes obnoxious, their feeling toward the tax collectors was nothing short of loathing. To be a tax collector (or publican) in first-century Israel meant to be a traitor to your nation. Taxes were collected for the Roman government, and the Jews heartily despised the Roman government. Jews who chose to collect taxes were in alliance with the hated government of the occupying soldiers, and a pagan government at that; and those who worked for and with the Roman tyrants were enemies not only of their own people but—so most Jews reasoned—of God as well.

Most tax collectors seemed to be dishonest. The system encouraged fraud. The Roman tax structure ran much like our modern franchise system of business. Having purchased the rights to a taxing unit, it was up to the collector to see how much money he could make from it. Such a system was a test of character. Most collectors found great profit in taking advantage of the taxpayers.

Thankful Not to Be Like Others ▪

Read Luke 18:9-14. Where was the Pharisee? What is the significance of his place of prayer?

Thankful Not to Be Like Others

Jesus' description of the Pharisee rang true to what the people had observed. "The Pharisee, standing by himself, was praying" (18:11); folks in the crowd nodded appreciatively, for many of the Pharisees frequently conducted themselves in that fashion. They often had an aloof quality about them. And

What was the nature of the Pharisee's prayer? Was there anything wrong with his prayer?

Is it possible to have a "wrong prayer"? If so, what prayers would be considered wrong or inappropriate or displeasing to God? Why, do you think?

What other spiritual practices besides prayer did the Pharisee observe? What is their meaning in this story? How might those practices enhance the Pharisee's standing in the faith community?

when the Pharisee in the story thanked God that he was "not like other people: thieves, rogues, adulterers, or even like this tax collector" (18:11), those in the crowd who were fair had to admit that what the Pharisee was saying was true. As far as basic, outward morality was concerned, the Pharisees were generally beyond reproach. The average person could see that the Pharisees did all that the law required and that they were therefore deserving of admiration. Yet somehow, most ordinary people did not really want to be like the Pharisees.

The unattractiveness in the manner of some of the Pharisees is well illustrated in the next sentence in the Pharisee's prayer: "I fast twice a week; I give a tenth of all my income" (18:12). Pharisees were so scrupulous about their tithing that they even measured out a tenth of the spices they raised.

And as for fasting twice a week, it is likely the Pharisee was referring to what was a common Pharisaical practice of fasting on Mondays and Thursdays. Those were the market days, and Jerusalem was filled with great numbers of shoppers in from the country. Some of the Pharisees made the most of these days by whitening their faces and wearing shabby clothing that would convey the appearance of spiritual humility. This practice helps us understand what Jesus had in mind when he said, "And whenever you fast, do not look dismal, like the hypocrites.... But when you fast, put oil on your head and wash your face, so that your fasting may be seen not by others but by your Father who is in secret" (Matthew 6:16-18).

But we must be careful in criticizing the Pharisee, for in his rigid conduct he is a better person than many of us. Tithing is commonly observed by a large percentage of church members. But as an ordained minister, I have to remind myself to tithe also on the rental value of the parsonage, which is a much bigger item than spices. And how many of us fast twice a week, or even twice a month? Before we smile condescendingly on the Pharisee, let us confess our frequent lack of attention to details of the Christian life.

Recognizing One's Sinfulness ■

Where did the tax collector choose as his place to pray? How is this different from the Pharisee's choice?

What was the publican's attitude toward and posture for prayer? How was it different from the Pharisee's?

What was the tax collector's prayer? What is the implication of "sinner" in his prayer?

What did Jesus mean about the publican being "justified"?

Have you ever felt like such a sinner? Did anything ever happen to help you feel justified?

Recognizing One's Sinfulness

The tax collector's approach came from the opposite extreme. He went off alone, as if acknowledging that others would find his presence offensive. He felt he could not even lift his eyes heavenward. Instead, he beat on his chest in painful recognition of his unworthiness as he wept, "God, be merciful to me, a sinner!" (Luke 18:13). Students of Greek remind us that what he said was not simply that he was *a* sinner but that he was *the* sinner, as if to suggest that he felt no one had grieved God as deeply as he had.

As Jesus described the tax collector, some in the crowd were probably moved by the publican's deep distress; but perhaps others said, "Such a prayer is appropriate for such a thief."

Those sure of the publican's guilt must have been shocked by Jesus' conclusion to his story: "I tell you, this man went down to his home justified rather than the other" (18:14). Such a word seemed to turn upside down all the cherished ideas about religion. Most of the people probably felt that the Pharisee, even if not appealing to their tastes, was nevertheless what God expected a person to be. How could a tax collector—a traitor to the Jewish people and all that they held dear—be more acceptable to God than a person who worked so earnestly at his religion?

How indeed? The answer is in the parable itself, beginning with the writer's word of introduction: This parable is meant for those who trust in themselves, believing that they are righteous; those persons who despise others. Such feelings of superiority coupled with a lack of tolerance for others is a deadly combination, and the two attitudes usually go together.

When we trust most in ourselves and in our own goodness, we are most likely to condemn others; for surely if we trust in God completely, we are not as apt to feel severely judgmental. Is not trusting only in one's own righteousness the very meaning of the ugly word *self-righteousness*? If the righteousness we have is a product of our own efforts, it becomes a matter of pride; and we then get the feeling that we can look down on those who haven't attained such goodness.

But if we realize that our righteousness is a gift from God, we have no reason for boasting and no reason to feel superior to someone who may have less. After all, if my own righteousness is something I have obtained by the grace of God, how can I feel superior to someone who apparently has less?

At first glance, the Pharisee in his prayer seems to be giving thanks to God; indeed, he himself thinks so, for he says, "God, I thank you." But before long we see that his prayer is more a declaration of self-congratulation than of thanksgiving. He is letting God know how fortunate God is to have this Pharisee on the heavenly team.

Focusing on Ourselves

By definition, prayer should have God as its focus. But our prayers can easily slip into a mood in which God is peripheral to us. This happens easily when we are asking God for help, for at such a time our mind is likely to be absorbed with our need rather than

---

What is the difference between self-righteousness and righteousness?

What is the source of righteousness? Are you or could you be righteous? Explain.

Focusing on Ourselves

On what did the Pharisee's prayers focus? What should be the focus of prayer?

with the God to whom we pray. The Pharisee in this story fell into the pit of self-centeredness even as he gave thanks. He was not so much impressed with God's goodness as he was with his own achievements. Woven throughout his prayer is a tone that says, "See what my own hand has accomplished."

Of course, the deadliest quality in the Pharisee's prayer is its meanness of spirit. Not only did he compare himself generally with "others"; but when he singled out the tax collector and thanked God that he was better than this poor soul, the unkindness in his attitude is repulsive.

After all, tax collectors were the most despised people in the populace. We realize as much when we recall that their name was always linked with "sinners." How could the Pharisee possibly feel any pride in saying that he was better than a tax collector, of all people? A similar situation would be a college graduate boasting that he knows more than a fourth grader. You want to reply, "Well, I should surely hope so!"

The Pharisee might have seemed to make a point if he had been able to compare himself favorably with some fellow Pharisee, but to exalt himself by downgrading one who was already so low seems like nothing other than a kind of spiritual brutality.

The possibility of offering a good prayer when we are despising some other human being is almost nil. To despise another is to show contempt for the One who made that other person and who loves him or her. When I express contempt for another human being, I am critical of God's taste; for God has declared God's own love for this person. Who am I to be contemptuous of someone God loves? How do I justify my opinion over against that of our Lord?

Have you ever compared yourself to others as the Pharisee did? If so, what has been the result? What effect did it have on your faith?

What happens when we downgrade another to exalt ourselves? Have you ever been put down so someone else could feel good? If so, how did it feel to you? What would be an appropriate response of faith? What did you do?

In Comparison With God

In Comparison With God ■

What is the best (and only) standard for our faith?

Look up Matthew 5:48. What does it tell us to do? What does this mean?

What does it mean to you to be called to a life of godliness? Do you think you are called to such a life? If so, do you try to live out that call? How?

How did the Pharisee, a person so earnest about religion, get so far off the track? He did so by comparing himself with the wrong standard. Nothing in authentic biblical religion urges us to compare ourselves with our fellow human beings. Godly people can be an incentive to us, but even they can never be our final standard. Jesus put it simply and directly: "Be perfect, therefore, as your heavenly Father is perfect" (Matthew 5:48), meaning that we should love as graciously and as tolerantly as God. Here is our standard, our only standard.

And when we compare ourselves with God, we find no reason to boast. The late William Barclay, the beloved Scottish Bible teacher, recalled a train trip through the Yorkshire moors as he traveled from Scotland to England. He saw a whitewashed cottage that seemed almost to shine with its lovely whiteness. A few days later, he made the return trip. Meanwhile, snow had fallen. When the train came to the little white cottage, Dr. Barclay was startled to see that now its whiteness seemed drab and almost gray compared with the fresh whiteness of the snow. Everything depends, he said, on what we compare ourselves with. When we set our lives alongside the life of our Lord, our best human efforts fall far short.

And that is the lesson the Pharisee had somehow missed. He had no business comparing himself with the tax collector or with anyone else. Like every true believer, he had been called to a life of *godliness*. We somehow forget that *godliness* means to be as much like God as possible. Such a quest is a lifelong pursuit.

But if the Pharisee was off the mark, we should pause momentarily to recognize that

---

he was no more in danger of missing the point than was the tax collector. Helmut Thielicke, the great German pastor-teacher, noted that it is just as possible for us to fool ourselves in our abjectness as in our pride. That is, he said, we can "make an accomplishment of [our] humility."

Such apparent humility expresses itself in such phrases as, "I know I've never amounted to much, but..." And again, "I may not be perfect, but at least I'm honest with myself about my shortcomings." Good! Such honesty is a good beginning place for true holiness, but it is not a very good place to stop. We can wrap ourselves in a kind of mock humility—and be quite sincere about it—and then let that confession of our shortcomings become an excuse for never becoming any better.

Apparently the publican never allowed himself to slip into such self-deception. He felt the weight of his unworthiness deeply and wished to be relieved of the load. Impressively, God was the sole object of his concern. He made no comparisons with anyone around him; his attention was focused exclusively and passionately on God against whom he had sinned.

A cynic might note that the tax collector was not in a position to make a favorable comparison as the Pharisee was. Who, after all, was worse than he was? Almost any one of us can locate someone who seems lower on the spiritual pecking order if we are interested in identifying such a person. The point is this: The tax collector was not seeking such a person. He was absorbed with only one issue, the state of his own soul before God.

So the tax collector went away justified, Jesus said, and the Pharisee did not. To be

What are some examples of false piety that one might use to try to dodge having to grow and take risks as a Christian?

Have you ever tried any of these tactics? If so, what was the result? If you worked successfully to resist the temptation, what was the result? What does this mean for your faith now?

How would you describe the state of your own soul before God now?

justified meant to be accepted by God or to be right with God. At this point, the crowd was probably more than a little confused. They could not help thinking the Pharisee deserved more of God's favor. They were sure he was better than the majority of the audience, comprised of honest people of the land; so surely he was better than a tax collector.

The listeners must have felt that Jesus was turning upside down all their notions of religion. Some people had the impression that Jesus held tax collectors and sinners in higher regard than those persons in the community most honored for their piety.

What Really Matters ■

According to this parable, what really matters? What matters most about it to you?

What Really Matters

But in truth, Jesus was only saying what the Hebrew prophets had declared: God is looking for inward truth, not for outward show. This lesson is as old as Cain and Abel. After all, both of them went through the same religious formula of making an offering to God. On the surface they were equally acceptable. The difference, the New Testament Book of Hebrews tells us, was an inner one. Abel made a better sacrifice to God because he was marked by faith (Hebrews 11:4).

How can "good people" protect themselves against the sins of the Pharisees? Is it possible to pursue a standard of excellence without becoming critical of those who do not pursue or reach such a standard?

Jesus closed the parable with a sharp warning: "All who exalt themselves will be humbled, but all who humble themselves will be exalted" (Luke 18:14). If we will not face ourselves honestly before God, the realities of life itself will intrude and clarify the issue. We cannot forever hide under a cloak of superficial religion.

We are sometimes struck by the fact that the people who give the most ardent witness to their faith in Christ are those who have been saved from the more obvious and dramatic forms of sin. Like the tax collector, they know how much they need the mercy of God. Those of us raised in the church often have more difficulty sensing the extent of our need.

What place, if any, does feeling "unworthy" have in living a faithful life?

But such a realization is not impossible. Many of our forebears in the faith led lives of great personal discipline, but their contributions to the hymnody of their day often reveal their sense of unworthiness before God and the need of divine forgiveness. They were not morbid or depressed about it, but they realized their capacity for sin and their need of forgiveness and strength from God. Grace, you see, is for "nice people" too.

What is the role of grace in prayer? in daily living?

How can any human being hope to come before God with anything other than a sense of need? Each time a congregation sings the words "Holy, holy, holy," this experience is a reminder that the character of God is the standard by which we approach life and that it is a demanding standard. If we see that fact clearly, we will pray as the tax collector did. And remembering the promises offered us in Jesus Christ, we will give thanks.

The Parable and Me ■

What is the main point of the parable?

The Parable and Me

Few parables strike closer to home for most of us than this one. The more pious we are, the more we are likely to need the message. For ironically, it is in the very earnestness of our quest for God and for honorable living that we are made susceptible to the possibilities of self-righteousness. As we strive to do good and to be good, we can easily become impressed with our own goodness; and when we do, we lose the very righteousness we seek.

So you and I are probably more in danger of committing the sins of the Pharisee than those of the tax collector. As earnest and well-meaning as we are, we can slip unconsciously into a mood of self-congratulation and its near cousin, self-righteousness.

If we succumb to this false pride, we will have gotten just enough religion to protect ourselves against God. One has the feeling that the Pharisees of Jesus' day were not intentionally hypocritical people. The Pharisees were people who desired lives of true quality. But somehow some of the Pharisees began to think of themselves more than of the God whose favor they intended to pursue; and, wrapped up in themselves, they came slowly to feel that they could be good without God's help.

The parable gives fair warning to you and me. We must be on our guard lest we fall into the subtle trap of self-righteousness without our being aware of what is happening.

What does it mean, do you think, to have "just enough religion to protect ourselves against God"?

Do you think you can be good without God's help? Explain?

If you wish, have a time of prayer to make or to reaffirm your commitment to Jesus Christ.

Close With Prayer ■

Join hands for this closing prayer:

We give you thanks, our Heavenly Friend, for accepting us as we are. When we come as tax collectors, burdened by the sense of our sins, you receive us with mercy and patience; and when, like a Pharisee, we appear with boasting, you wait with patience for us to receive better insight into our own shortcomings. Help us, we pray, to partake of your same gracious spirit, so that we shall accept others with patience, love, and compassion. And may we, as time goes by, grow together into the likeness of our Savior. In Jesus' name we pray. Amen.

The Nobleman and the Pounds
Luke 19:11-26

Session Focus ■

We Christians are an active people, busy in work and community as well as in church. Our focus therefore should not be on accelerating activity but on rethinking our calling as Christians and also on coming to a new understanding of our gifts and how to use them effectively.

Session Objective ■

Group members should gain from studying this chapter a thoughtful commitment to service, recognizing that service is sometimes perilous; but we should also feel new hopefulness about our capacity to be profitable servants, especially with the knowledge that God wants us to succeed in our divine mission.

Session Preparation ■

Appropriately, this parable is the concluding unit in our study because it is a call to renewed discipleship. In preparing for this session, consider ways the material can be made effective both in the per-

We human beings are a gifted lot. Most of us never begin to use or even to recognize the extent of our abilities and talents. Indeed, the people who achieve the most, in most instances, are probably not those who are most gifted, but instead those who recognize their talents enough to celebrate them, develop them to their potential, and use them effectively.

The Bible teaches that our gifts are a divine trust. They are, as indicated by the word we use, *gifts*; and God is the great Benefactor.

But God is not an undemanding Benefactor. God expects a worthy return on the divine investment. Jesus taught that we will each someday face an accounting. As a matter of fact, the accounting will be a little like our classroom experience: We will face not only a final examination but also a series of interim exams. And the interim exams (and the "pop" quizzes), as with all good educational endeavors, are intended to make us fully prepared for that big final examination that will determine if we pass—or fail.

God Invests in Us

During his ministry Jesus apparently told several stories to illustrate the issue of our

Session Outline ■

Open with prayer, asking God to open our eyes to the talents we have and to give us the courage to use them in God's service.

God Invests in Us ■
What are the talents that you bring to your community?

What responsibility do you feel as a steward of what God has provided?

What is a "pound" worth in our currency?

What was the noble's direction to each of the servants?

Some Dissent in the Ranks ■

Read Luke 19:11-26. What happens in this story?

What might have been the historical backdrop to this story?

sonal life of class members and in the life of the congregation and the community. Apply your knowledge of the individuals and the community involved to make this thoughtful and prayerful analysis.

responsibility as talented stewards. The story we are considering from the Gospel of Luke is similar in many ways to a story that appears in Matthew 25. Details are different, but the bottom line is essentially the same: God invests generously in us human creatures (indeed, God invests in the whole universe, animate and inanimate); and God expects a worthy return on what has been given to each one of us.

So Jesus told the crowd a story. A nobleman went into a faraway place to receive the kingdom that had been promised him. His absence was to be a relatively long one, so he called in ten of his servants and gave them each a pound. A pound represented about three months' wages; you can translate that fact into your own style of finances. The nobleman's instructions were simple, straightforward, and trusting: "Do business with these until I come back."

Some Dissent in the Ranks

Jesus interjects at this point that the citizens of the nobleman's area hated him and sent a delegation after him to insist that they did not want him to reign over them. This episode apparently reflects an actual historical incident.

When Herod the Great died in 4 B.C., he left his kingdom to be divided between three assistants, one of whom, Archelaus, was to rule over Judea. The people of Judea did not want him, however; and when he went to Rome to persuade Augustus Caesar to give him his inheritance, the people of Judea sent a delegation of fifty men to Rome to let Augustus know their objections. Augustus responded with a kind of compromise, confirming Archelaus in his inheritance, but not giving him the actual title of king. Without a doubt many people in Jesus' audience thought of this event from their history as he told the parable.

We Are Expected to Invest for God

We Are Expected to Invest for God ■

When the nobleman in the parable returned with his new authority, he called in his servants to seek an accounting. The first servant had a jubilant report; he had made ten pounds with the one entrusted him. The second also had done well, gaining five pounds with his pound. In both cases, the nobleman responded with generosity. He assigned ten cities to the first man and five to the second, judging that because they had been effective in handling a relatively small trust, they could be counted on to do a much greater thing.

But another servant was not as confident. He had kept the pound "wrapped up in a piece of cloth, for I was afraid of you," he explained, "because you are a harsh man; you take what you did not deposit, and reap what you did not sow" (Luke 19:20-21).

The landowner was incensed. He hated both the fearfulness that motivated the third servant and his reasoning. "I will judge you by your own words," he answered. "You knew, did you, that I was a harsh man, taking what I did not deposit and reaping what I did not sow? Why then did you not put my money into the bank? Then when I returned, I could have collected it with interest" (9:22-23).

Then the landowner did an apparently cruel thing. He instructed those who were nearby that they should take this third servant's pound and give it to the one who already had ten. Some of the people protested that the first servant already had ten; why give him more? But the landowner replied, "I tell you, to all those who have, more will be given; but from those who have nothing, even what they have will be taken away" (19:26).

Taking Care of the Master's Business

Our interpretation of this strange and dramatic parable ought to begin with the background setting. Jesus told the parable, Luke explains, "because he was near Jerusalem, and because they supposed that the kingdom of God was to appear immediately" (19:11). The disciples were of the opinion that Jesus was going to Jerusalem in order to claim his kingdom. But Jesus was trying to warn them instead that they were facing a long wait.

This is a parable, then, for servants who are taking care of the Master's business while the Kingdom tarries. We are trusted servants, each of us equipped with some special talent. The Master has not put us under strict regulations as to how we shall use our gifts. To the contrary, he has left us not only with the choice as to how we shall use our gifts, but even as to whether we will use them.

But the gifts themselves constitute a calling. To have a talent is to have a responsibility. In life's final reckoning, no one will be able to say that there was nothing he or she could do. All of us have gifts, and all of us are expected to put them to use.

Sadly, most of us are not properly conscious of our gifts. We are inclined to notice and thus to envy those more obvious talents in such areas as music, public address, and leadership. Yet if each of us would make a list of the people who have meant the most in our lives, our lists would not be dominated by people in these prominent categories. Life is touched and enriched in a wide variety of ways, and only a few of these ways ever catch the public eye.

Taking Care of the Master's Business ■

What does the parable suggest about taking care of the master's business? Who is the master?

Who are the servants? What is the master's attitude toward the servants in the interpretation of the parable?

If God has left to us the choice of whether and how to use our gifts, what responsibility does that place on us, if any?

Do you regard your gifts as a calling that takes on a certain amount of responsibility? Explain.

In recent years ministers have begun to speak more about the gifts of the Spirit. The emphasis began with charismatic groups who concentrated particularly on certain of the more spectacular demonstrations of faith. Then the realization came that the New Testament refers to numbers of gifts beyond those mentioned in the fourteenth chapter of First Corinthians. Sometimes one gets the feeling that God's gifts are as numerous and specialized as our fingerprints. Each of us has specific and wonderful contributions to make to our time and place.

What gifts in others have been most beneficial to you? Which of your gifts have been most beneficial to others?

Different but Equal

As Jesus presents the issues in this parable, all the workers were equally endowed. That is an insight worth noting. One must assume that is the way it is in God's sight. Different as our talents may be, each is appropriate to the owner; and each owner will be judged simply for what she or he does with what is given. In that sense we are utterly equal. The Master looks for us to do what we can with what we have.

But how is it that the first two persons mentioned in the parable put their talents to such effective use, while the third person was a failure? We are not told specifically how it is that these two workers ventured forth full of energy to achieve. But we are told why the third one failed, and I expect we can reason that the others succeeded for possessing the opposite characteristic. "I was afraid of you," the third man said.

Different but Equal ■

Do you think the servants or workers in the parable were equally endowed? Explain. Are all workers or servants now equally endowed with talents and abilities? with spiritual gifts? Explain.

Would you characterize the third servant as a failure? Why or why not?

Paralyzed by Fear

So it was fear that destroyed the prospects of this otherwise talented person, fear that prevented him from using the gifts that had been entrusted to him. Fear commonly interferes with many human endeavors. Many of

Paralyzed by Fear ■

How does fear interfere with human endeavor? How have your plans, commitments, or dreams been interrupted by fear? What, if anything, did you do about it?

What part, if any, did your faith play in dealing with or confronting your fears?

us can look back on a lifetime of friendships and of observing human beings and can recall any number of people who never achieved their potential simply because they were afraid to venture.

Fear kept a friend of mine from going to college. He did not think he could manage it financially, and he was afraid to make the leap. I know a woman who wanted all her life to start a little business of her own, and her idea was a good one. But she never acted upon her dream because she was afraid of failing. Many a church has settled in to serve only a fraction of the people it might because its members were afraid to risk enlarging their building or their parking lot.

Do you agree or disagree that "fear paralyzes while faith liberates"? Explain.

The late Harry Emerson Fosdick said that fear paralyzes while faith empowers; fear imprisons while faith liberates. Those words surely apply to the persons in our parable. Emotionally, the third servant was paralyzed and in prison. He could have done no less with his pound if he had been behind prison bars. He might as well not have had a pound, because it was useless to him.

Is fear a sin? Explain.

Something in us may argue that the man should not be blamed for having his fears. After all, fear is not a sin, is it? Fear may not be properly defined as an act of sin. But surely it is one of the by-products of the fact of sin in our world. Fear frustrates the purposes of God as surely as does hate, bitterness, or despair. Fear prevents us human beings from accomplishing God's purposes, and—as in the case of the servant—robs us of our divine potential.

Overcoming Fear

Overcoming Fear ■

Review Hebrews 11 for examples of how persons of faith overcame obstacles, or fears, to accomplish God's purposes. How would you phrase the opposite of some of these examples, other than the ones mentioned already?

For fear is the opposite of faith, just as hate and indifference are the opposite of love. When we fear, we lose faith; and when faith is strong, it drives out fear. You can see the issue clearly if you will examine the great faith chapter, Hebrews 11, and see how precisely the results will be reversed if fear is substituted for faith. "By faith Noah . . . built an ark" (11:7) becomes "By fear Noah was discouraged from building an ark." "By faith Abraham obeyed when he was called to set out for a place that he was to receive as an inheritance" (11:8); "by fear," it would read, "Abraham was prevented from striking out on his pilgrimage."

Fear is our act of believing the adversary rather than believing God. Faith holds out a promised land to us, and fear paralyzes us so that we cannot enter in.

Most of us are familiar with the little saying,

Do you believe this little saying? Has it been true in your experience? Why?

Fear knocked at the door.
Faith answered.
No one was there.

This is a true saying, and it demonstrates so well that fear and faith are precise opposites. If, as the writer of Hebrews 11:6 said, "without faith it is impossible to please God," then fear is our enemy because fear displaces faith.

Can you please God without faith and without effectively using your gifts and talents? Give reasons for your response.

What Might Have Been

The two successful servants were not necessarily better men than the third. In truth, we will never know how good the third man was or how great his potential may have been. It is altogether possible that this third servant could have surpassed both the others.

But we never hear stories of what might have been. We read with excitement the tales of those who venture grandly and who succeed, and we read at times of those who venture and who fail. But history carries no

What Might Have Been ■

Have you ever been trapped by the dangers of the "what might have been" thinking or behavior? What does this tell you about the role of faith in tapping your greatest potential?

record of those who never tried. And it is fear that keeps us from trying, fear that persuades us to wrap our gifts and our potential in a cloth and to bury them.

Reward for Productivity

Reward for ■
Productivity
The nobleman seems quite lacking in patience and sympathy. Do you think he did right, given the harsh realities of the world? Explain.

Thinking of this story as a parable about using our faith, do you think God is so impatient?

Is there a point at which God's patience wears out or wears thin? If so, how would you describe that point?

In the divine economy, do you think it is fair or reasonable that the one who has much (or has been faithful in much) should get much more? Explain?

Should the one who has done least well get the greatest chance to do better or have to lose what little he or she has? How do you think God looks on that now?

In the parable the judgment that follows may seem harsh. The landowner expressed no sympathy or understanding. "If you were smart enough to know that I'm a severe man who expects a return on all his investments, why didn't you at least put out my money to interest?" The landowner never said, "I'm sorry about your fearfulness." We live in a world that will collapse if fear becomes the dominant force. Therefore, fear is to be dreaded like a plague.

Instead, the nobleman instructed his attendants to take the carefully wrapped pound and give it to the man who already had ten (and who was now about to become supervisor for ten cities). When others pointed out that the first man had all he needed, Jesus answered, "To all those who have, more will be given."

Jesus is not declaring a judgment; he is simply reporting what kind of world we live in. Our universe operates this way. The musician who practices becomes a still better musician, and the athlete who exercises regularly becomes still more muscular and athletic. By contrast, those who wrap their skill or strength in a cloth of unproductivity find, when they want to use it, that its power has diminished, perhaps even disappeared. The whole universe is on the side of faith and action. When we retire into a shell, we are running against the order of things.

We ought to pay attention therefore to the hard words in this parable. When the landowner confesses that he is, indeed, a "harsh man" who expects a return on his investment, we can rightly note that life is just such a severe taskmaster.

Nature is geared to productivity. The forces of nature recycle fallen leaves and animal refuse as fertilizer. The trees take impure elements from the air and transform them into fresh air for our breathing. Nature is fiercely economical. God endows our world so abundantly, indeed, so lavishly; yet God expects the world's resources to conserve and to be conserved.

God's Generosity

God's Generosity ■

Do you think God's "rewards are all out of proportion to the achievement"? Explain.

But see also the boundless generosity of our Lord. To those who did their work well, the landowner spoke exuberantly: "You have been faithful over a few things; I will make you ruler over many." A servant turns three months' wages into a tenfold success—money representing thirty months—and the landowner makes him a sub-governor, ruling over ten cities. Not only does this man receive a reasonably large sum of money and responsibility for a small business, he also becomes a kind of prince in the kingdom. The rewards are all out of proportion to the achievement. So it is with the goodness and grace of God.

Helmut Thielicke, a theologian and biblical scholar, felt that this parable is telling us that God demands an all-out decision. We must either let God be Lord of life, Thielicke said, or we must throw Christianity on the ash heap. But we are not given the alternative of wrapping up God in our handkerchiefs. Not having that as an alternative disturbs us.

We are inclined to look rather sympathetically at the third servant and say, "Well, at least he didn't lose the money." But to such

Does the third servant deserve pity, in your opinion? Why or why not? Is his passivity a danger to the faith? to the community? Explain your response.

reasoning our Lord might answer in the language of the Book of Revelation, "I wish that you were either cold or hot. So, because you are lukewarm, and neither cold nor hot, I am about to spit you out of my mouth" (Revelation 3:15-16).

Next to rejecting Jesus Christ, no doubt the worst sin we can commit is to waste our life. After all, to waste our life is to scorn the Lord who gave us this priceless gift. J. B. Phillips, the Anglican rector who left us with such a beautiful translation of the New Testament, was unhappy with a hymn he learned in his youth. It began with the line, "O to be nothing, nothing. . . ." Dr. Phillips said that you could search all through the New Testament and you would never find an endorsement for that point of view. If ever a book taught people to be "something, something," he said, it is the New Testament.

These Scriptures insist that we are made far more full of joy and daring and life with Christ than ever we could be without him. God enlarges and electrifies life. Surely God does not want us to turn it into a receptacle of defeat and retreat.

What, do you think, does the New Testament teach you to be? Is it a sin to think of "being nothing"? or is it the goal of humility? Explain.

The Dangers of Hoarding Our Gifts

The Dangers of Hoarding Our Gifts ■

I confess that I used to feel sorry for the third servant in the story. It seemed to me that he was too harshly reprimanded by his master. But as I look back on my own life and regret that I have not used it more effectively and as I see how little most of us make of the gifts God bestows on us so abundantly, I have come to feel sorry for the Master. He invests so much in us, trusts us with such unexcelled riches; and all that he asks is that we "earn something" with what has been given to us. How can we disappoint the Master so?

Our answer has to come in our acts of

What are the risks involved in using your gifts for God? What, in your experience, have been the blessings?

If you wish to make or to reaffirm your commitment to Jesus Christ, offer a prayer that dedicates you and your gifts to the faith community.

faith. We will not hoard life in fear. Instead, we will believe in the One who said, "For those who want to save their life will lose it, and those who lose their life for my sake, and for the sake of the gospel, will save it" (Mark 8:35). The Lord who gambled so fearlessly on us deserves nothing less in our response.

The Parable and Me

We can react to this parable correctly if we appreciate the extent of God's love for us. Each of us is offered the grand gift of life itself and the still grander gift of the prospect of eternal life. These gifts come without our proving any merit or offering any plan as to how we will use them. The Master simply trusts us to put the priceless gifts to work. We could not be loved more or trusted more.

But such trust has a price. In studying this parable, we want to examine our hearts and talents—and even more, our time. What are we doing with these gifts? Are we inclined to live too carefully, guarding these treasures as if they were ours alone and not putting them to work for God?

At this point, most of us are guilty of selling ourselves short. And in the process, we sell God's purposes short. It is not a matter of our doing more but of our coming to appreciate more fully that God really can use us for eternal purposes. Our Lord's desire is to make us more fruitful and effective.

The Parable and Me

Do you think God trusts you? Why? Do you trust yourself to do God's will? Explain.

What might you have to change, if anything, to be the best steward for God that you could be?

Close With Prayer

Pray together using this prayer:

Grant us, dear Master, a new vision of our divine potential. Help us to see how generously you have invested in us. Forgive us when we minimize your investments in our life; save us from the mistaken humility that prevents us from acknowledging your gifts to us. And help us, gracious Lord, to go into this week with a special sense of purpose and with high expectations. May we see that you want us to multiply the pounds that have been entrusted to us, and may we be filled with hope and faith in that realization. In the name of Jesus our Lord we pray. Amen.